AF572406

Botticelli's Witness

to muouerſi/ſe prima non ſi muoue la ragione. Entrai per lo camino alto: cioe profondo/chome diciamo alto mare et alto fiume: perche el primo camino fu per linferno cioe per la cognitione de uitii: equali ſono infimi: perche ſempre conſiſtono circa le choſe terrene. ET SILueſtro: perche chome dicemo nel principio epeccati naſcono dalla ſelua cioe dalla materia che e/elcorpo.

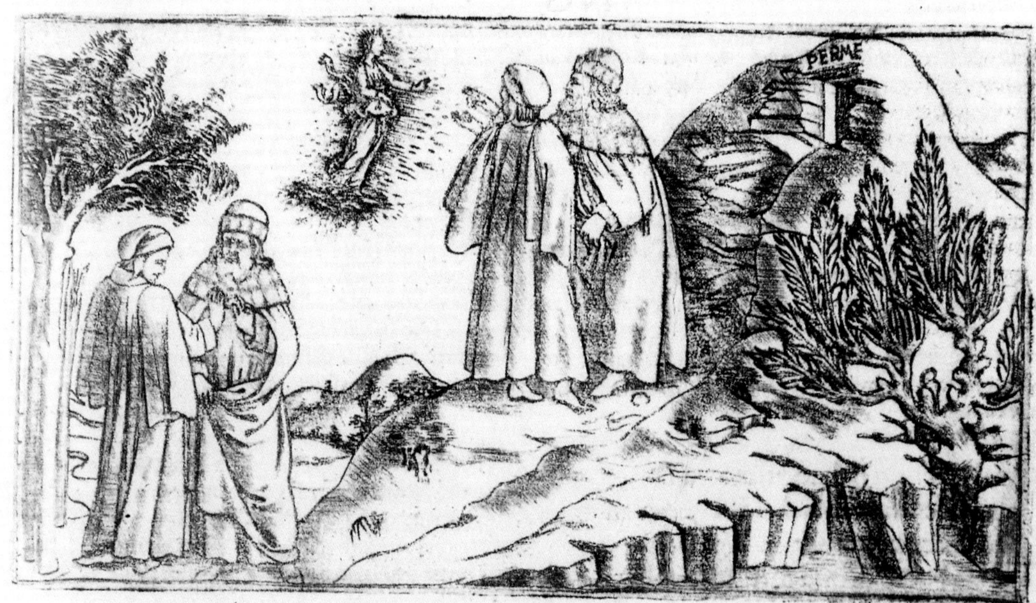

CANTO TERTIO DELLA PRIMA CANTICA

PEr me ſi ua nella citta dolente
per me ſi ua nelletherno dolore
per me ſi ua tra laperduta gente
Iuſtitia moſſe el mio alto factore
fecemi la diuina poteſtate
la ſomma ſapientia el primo amore
Dinanzi a me nonfur choſe create
ſe non etherne et io etherno duro
laſciate ogni ſperanza uoi chentrate
Queſte parole di colore obſcuro
uidio ſcripte al ſommo duna porta
perchio maeſtro el ſenſo lor me duro.

SOno alchuni equali credonoche edue primi capitoli ſieno ſtati inluoghi di proemio: et queſto terzo ſia el principio della narratione. Maſe conſiderremo chon diligentia tutta la materia/facilmente ſi puo prouare che la narratione comincia nel primo capitolo: et nel uerſo Io non ui ſo ben dire chomio uentrai. Imperoche Danthe narra in queſta ſua peregrinatione eſſerſi ritrouato nella ſelua: et hauere ſmarrito la uia Eſſerſi condocto appie del monte. Et dipoi eſſerſi addirizato uerſo el ſole per erto camino elquale lo conduceua aſaluamento ſe le tre fiere non laueſſino ripincto al baſſo. Et finalmente ridocto quaſi al fondo hauere hauuto el ſoccorſo di Virgilio et dalle tre donne. Et p leſue parole eſſer pſuaſo laſciādo el corto ādare del mōte ſeguitarlo per linferno et purgatorio: laqual uia ſanza ſiniſtro intoppo lo puo conducere al cielo. Ilche ſignifica quello che gia diſopra habbiamo dimoſtro. Et ſe alchuno diceſſi che in amendue queſti canti molte choſe ſcriue conle quali capta ben uolētia et attētione et docilita: Enon ſi uieta che ī ogni pte del poema non ſi poſſi fare queſto. Anzi maximamēte ſirichiede allo ſcriptore che le capti douūque truoua occaſione di poterlo fare. Hora perche ſiamo gia al puncto chel poeta deſcende nellinferno. Giudico ſa utile exprimere che choſa ſia inferno: et in quanti modi ſi dica alchuno ſcendere allinferno. Inferno adunque e/linfima: et baſſa parte del mondo/decto inferno da queſta dictione infra che ſignifica diſocto: Ne ſolamente dal popolo di dio e/poſto lonferno: Ma anchora da molti poeti: et maxime da Homero da Virgilio. Ouidio. Statio: et Claudiano: Et molto piu egregiamente dal principe de philoſophi Platone/Coſtui incritone nel qual libro induce Socrate diſputante della immortalita dellanimo/dimoſtra che lanime humane dopo la morte ſono giudicate ſecondo le loro colpe: et nellonferno tormentate inſino atanto che ſi purghino/ſe epeccati non ſono ſtati molto graui. Ma quelle che hanno commeſſo ſcelerateze enorme: et ſono impurgabili ſecondo lui/ſono mandate in luogho piu profondo decto tartaro et quiui ſono afflicte inetherno con grauiſſimi ſupplicii. La quale oppinione e/molto ſimile alla chriſtiana fede: et abbraccia lonferno el purgatorio: Et la maggior pte

Botticelli's Witness:

Changing Style in a Changing Florence

Laurence Kanter

Hilliard T. Goldfarb

James Hankins

Isabella Stewart Gardner Museum
Boston, Massachusetts

This catalogue is published to accompany the exhibition organized by the Isabella Stewart Gardner Museum.

"Botticelli's Witness: Changing Style in a Changing Florence"
Isabella Stewart Gardner Museum, Boston
January 24–April 6, 1997

Cover:
Sandro Botticelli
Madonna and Child with an Angel
Isabella Stewart Gardner Museum, Boston
Photo: David Bohl

Frontispiece: After a design by Sandro Botticelli
Dante and Virgil, with the Vision of Beatrice
Fogg Art Museum, Harvard University Art Museums

Published by The Trustees of the Isabella Stewart Gardner Museum
Two Palace Road, Boston, Massachusetts 02115

Photography credits: Figs. 1–3, Galleria degli Uffizi, Florence, courtesy of The Bridgeman Art Library, London; Fig. 4, The National Gallery, London; Figs. 6 and 7, Accademia Carrara, Bergamo; Cats. 1, 2a, 3, 5, 10, and Appendix Cantos I–XIX © Isabella Stewart Gardner Museum, Boston (photos 1, 3, and 5 by David Bohl, 2a by John Kennard, 10 by Clive Russ); Cats. 2b, 2c, 4, and 8 © The President and Fellows, Harvard College, Harvard University Art Museums; Fig. 5 © Harvard College Library, Photographic Services; Cats. 6, 7, and 9 courtesy of the Museum of Fine Arts, Boston.

Design: Higgins & Ross with Ruth Abrahams

Printing: LaVigne Press

ISBN 0-9648475-3-1

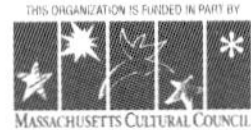

Contents

Preface

THE ART OF BOTTICELLI is very much at the heart of the Gardner Museum's collection. The artist's late masterpiece *The Tragedy of Lucretia* was the first major Italian Old Master painting purchased by Isabella Stewart Gardner and the first acquired through the advice of Bernard Berenson, the great art agent and connoisseur of the Italian Renaissance. The painting, bought in 1894 from the venerable Ashburnham collection in England, set the standard for Isabella Stewart Gardner's later acquisitions in early Italian painting. The Gardner's rich collection of Botticelli's works, encompassing paintings from his early period, maturity, and late style, established the parameters of our exploration in this exhibition.

Helped by generous loans from the collections of the Harvard University Art Museums and the Museum of Fine Arts, Boston, we have organized an exhibition that looks at the relationship between Botticelli's distinct yet changing visual "voice" and the turbulent society of late fifteenth-century Florence, in which he lived. Through a close study of the changes in his style, by the evidence of our eyes, we can understand changes in Botticelli's relations to the world around him. This is a way of looking at art that is as relevant to the art of this century as it is to art produced in the age of Lorenzo "il Magnifico" de' Medici.

It is part of the Gardner Museum's mission to bring the treasures of the past closer to the experience of today's viewers through a better understanding of their contexts. To this end, this catalogue is composed in three sections. In his introductory essay, Dr. Hilliard Goldfarb, our chief curator of collections and organizer of this exhibition, explores both the cultural context in which Botticelli's works were produced and the trajectory of the artist's career. The essay by Professor James Hankins, of the History Department at Harvard University, discusses the impact of Girolamo Savonarola and religious fundamentalism on Florence in the 1490s. Dr. Laurence Kanter, curator of the Lehman Collection at the Metropolitan Museum of Art in New York, has written both the catalogue entries and an historical survey of critical appraisal of the artist. The design of the catalogue bears the impress of our creative designer, Ruth Abrahams.

The exhibition itself was the labor of many, especially our registrar, Patrick McMahon, our exhibition designer, Michael Rizzo, and our education curator, Karen Croff Bates, who created, in collaboration with area teachers, innovative programs to engage local students in the exhibition. This undertaking, inspired by one of the most beloved artists of the Renaissance, has been a labor of love for all of us, and we hope that it will transport you, the viewer, to the complex and turbulent times that Botticelli witnessed in his life and art.

Anne Hawley, Director
Isabella Stewart Gardner Museum

Sandro Botticelli As Artist and Witness: An Overview

Hilliard T. Goldfarb

Ne'medesimi tempi del magnifico Lorenzo vecchio de' Medici, che fu veramente per le persone d'ingegno un secol d'oro, fiorì ancora Alessandro, chiamato all'uso nostro Sandro, e detto di Botticello . . .
—*Giorgio Vasari,* Le Vite, *1568*

The name Botticelli evokes in the popular imagination a golden age of Florence under the leadership of Lorenzo "il Magnifico" de' Medici (d. 1492); it also calls to mind visions of idealized, slim and linearly defined Madonnas and goddesses. Indeed, it suggests an aesthetic world remote from the daily realities of the artist's own times, a world more intellectual and spiritual than passionate. In reality, however, Botticelli's life (1445–1510) and artistic expression were bounded by political and social forces of great impetus and divergent direction. The Florentine artist, who hardly left Florence except for a brief stay in Rome (1481–1482), experienced the cataclysmic series of events between the years of republican oligarchy, governed by Cosimo the Elder de' Medici, and the anti-Medicean republican rule of the early years of the sixteenth century. In those years, Botticelli witnessed and responded to situations both eventful and grim in the history of the city. In both its subjects and styles, Botticelli's art speaks to us as a creatively inspired and compelling record of the experiences that so profoundly affected the times in which he lived.

A successful and prominent Florentine artist, with commissions from the Medici, the pope, and leading Florentine families and civic institutions, Botticelli was a celebrated creator of religious works as well as mythologies, histories, and portraits that were characterized by a lyrical idealization of figures. Yet, in the 1490s, Botticelli experienced the radical religious exhortation of the Dominican visionary Girolamo Savonarola, and in his late compositions his figures reflect a concern for clear, direct, sermon-like communication, becoming more agitated, moving with compulsion and a theatrical directness of emotion. The atmosphere of courtly grace and the softly modelled and idealized forms of his earlier style are gone, replaced by an impetuous intensity of feeling and a passionate expressiveness of figures. This impassioned style is particularly apparent in one extraordinary work in the current exhibition, the apocalyptic Crucifixion image *Saint Mary Magdalene at the Foot of the Cross* (Harvard University Art Museums, Cat. 8), which commonly has been interpreted as depicting the salvation of a repentent Florence as foretold in one of Savonarola's sermons.

Rather than present a comprehensive retrospective of Botticelli's works, this exhibition looks closely at several early, mature, and late works to see what they can tell us about historical change and changes in artistic style. Using Botticelli's work as a prism, we propose that connoisseurship—the formal, stylistic examination of works of art—can be a useful documentation and lens for understanding a culture, revealing the "spirit" of a period in ways not always accessible through archival documen-

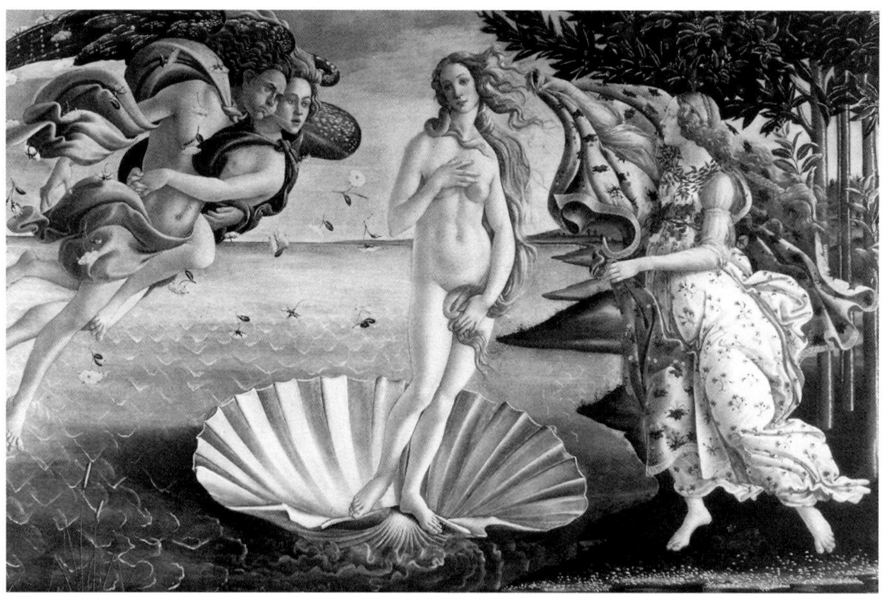

Figure 1. *The Birth of Venus.* Florence, Galleria degli Uffizi.

tation alone. The exhibition brings together ten works made by Botticelli or executed from his designs, and two works executed under his profound influence by contemporaries. (Remarkably, all these works come from three collections in Boston and Cambridge, Massachusetts.) By focusing on the work of one of the most popular and appealing artists of the Renaissance, one whose training, social contacts, and religious convictions put him at the center of a society in crisis, we seek to suggest ways of looking at art in other periods as well.

This catalogue includes an historical essay on Savonarola and his impact on Florentine society written by Professor James Hankins of Harvard University. That essay is followed by a summary of historical criticism and a brief biography of Botticelli (from a slightly different perspective from my own) written by the art historian Laurence Kanter. Dr. Kanter also contributed the catalogue entries for the objects included in the exhibition. It is the purpose of this introductory essay to broadly lay out the themes of this exhibition by presenting a brief overview of the artist's career and the concerns and interests that occupied his patrons and mentors.

In broad outline, then, what were the professional and societal contours of Botticelli's life? Unfortunately, one of the most indispensable sources for the life of Botticelli is also a biased one. Giorgio Vasari, the sixteenth-century artist, architect, and author, was also a courtier in the service of the Medici, and the later career of Botticelli, sympathetic as it appeared to Vasari to have been to the anti-Medicean faction, hardly disposed the biographer to an uncritical appraisal of Botticelli's life and work. (For example, Vasari misrepresents Botticelli's later life, suggesting that poor financial planning and adherence to the sect of Savonarola had reduced the artist to penury and that it was only through the intercession of Lorenzo and other wealthy men that he was rescued from starvation.) Nonetheless, the biography, especially the 1568 second edition, is a highly readable overview of Botticelli's life, animated with revealing anecdotes of his workshop activities.

I. The Life

We know that Sandro Botticelli (Alessandro di Mariano Filipepi) was born to Mariano, a Florentine tanner, the seventh of eight children and one of only four, all sons, to survive to adulthood. Indeed, his father was already fifty and his mother forty years old when he was born. All of these sons would be successful: Giovanni, the eldest, became a broker and banker; Antonio, a goldsmith; and Simone spent much of his career in the cloth business with the Rucellai family in Naples. Although in

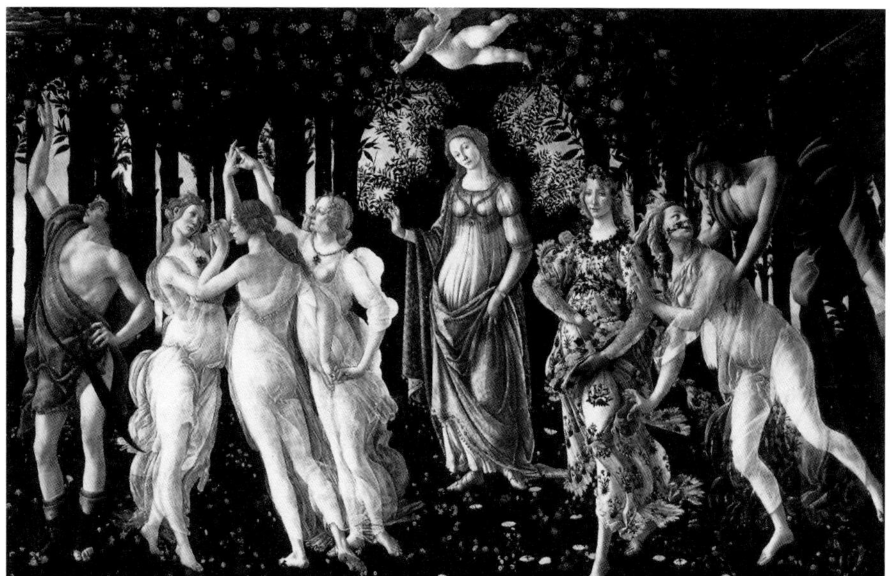

Figure 2. *Primavera.* Florence, Galleria degli Uffizi.

his tax records Mariano indicated that he was not a successful tanner, the evidence is that the family belonged to the middle class; by 1458, the family owned a country villa and had moved to an apartment in Florence owned by the prominent Rucellai family. In 1464 they were able to buy a house off the Borgo Ognissanti, near the prosperous Vespucci family, a family closely tied to the Medici; Sandro would live in this house from 1470 until his death. Although bright, the youth could not settle on a trade, and his father set him up, according to Vasari, with a goldsmith named Botticello. If, indeed, he studied with a goldsmith, it was probably with his brother Antonio. (A gold beater was called a *battigello* or *battiloro* and this might be the source of his nickname. On the other hand, Giovanni, who even after his marriage continued to live with the family and probably contributed to its financial success, himself apparently bore the nickname "Botticello" [little tub], and this is the more likely source of the name.)

Vasari tells us that Sandro, as a boy, was already devoted to drawing. Close ties existing at that time between goldsmiths and painters, he soon became interested in painting, and around 1461 his father took him to Fra Filippo Lippi (d. 1469), a highly successful and popular painter, whose loyal and prominent patrons included Cosimo de' Medici. The youth worked so diligently and imitated Lippi so well that his master, Vasari tells us, became fond of him, and while still young, Botticelli gained an independent reputation. As Ronald Lightbown, in his recent monograph (*Sandro Botticelli: Life and Work*, 1989), has observed, "From Lippi he learned the linear treatment of the human form that he was to use with so much more vigor, naturalism and expressiveness. The pointed oval faces with broad foreheads that recur in his art until the mid-1480s are Lippi's, as are the golden-headed impish boy angels of his tondos." He also acquired from Lippi an intimate style of painting holy figures that emphasizes their essential humanity through gesture and pose while conveying their majesty through a richness and detailing of costuming. Details such as the painting of nearly transparent material over brightly colored forms also derive from Lippi. Yet, even in his early work, Botticelli proved himself no imitator, preferring simpler compositions with fewer ornamental details in landscapes and interiors than characterize Lippi's work.

Botticelli's richly costumed, symbolic figure of Fortitude painted for the Mercanzia (trade law court) of Florence (1470, now at the Uffizi) is singled out by Vasari as a work of the artist's youth ("essendo giovanetto"). It is one of a series of Seven Virtues, otherwise executed by Piero del Pollaiuolo. While looking to the example of Pollaiuolo's *Virtues*, Botticelli's *Fortitude* yet reveals the impress of Lippi's models. Also dating from this period is the *Return of Judith to Bethulia* (ca. 1469–1470, Uffizi) and the Gardner Museum's *Madonna of the Eucharist* (ca. 1470, Cat. 1), which is included in the exhibition. In the *Fortitude* and the *Madonna of the Eucharist* Botticelli's style also has been influenced by a study of the greater volume and naturalism in the painted works of Pollaiuolo and Andrea del Verrocchio, both of

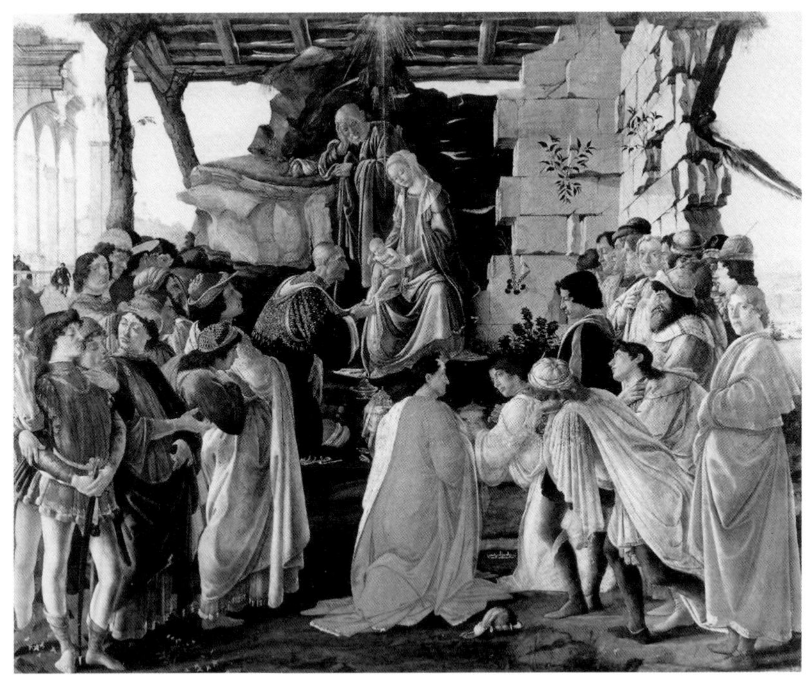

Figure 3. *Adoration of the Magi.* Florence, Galleria degli Uffizi.

whom were primarily sculptors. Verrocchio's influence on the Gardner painting is evident in the subtle modelling of figures in light and shadow and in the facial types of the Virgin and angel.

Besides painting religious and symbolic imagery for church and civic commissions, Botticelli also painted religious and mythological subjects for the Medici and other private patrons, including, Vasari says, "round pictures (tondi), and a goodly number of nude female figures." Among the latter he cites the *Birth of Venus* (1478, Uffizi, Fig. 1) and *Primavera* (1482, Uffizi, Fig. 2). He also executed decorative wall paintings. After listing a number of private commissions of religious art, Vasari notes that Botticelli's career was secured by the artistic success of his *Adoration of the Magi* (ca. 1475, Uffizi, Fig. 3). The work was commissioned by the merchant and Medici ally Guaspare del Lama for his chapel in Santa Maria Novella; it contains portraits, according to Vasari, of Cosimo de' Medici; Giuliano, his grandson and the brother of Lorenzo; and Giovanni, Cosimo's son. The painting is virtually a paean to the Medici family; it also includes portraits of Piero, Cosimo's other son and Lorenzo and Giuliano's father, and Lorenzo himself, as well as members of their cultural circle, including Angelo Poliziano, Giovanni Pico della Mirandola, and Botticelli himself (at the far right). According to Vasari, the success of this painting led to Botticelli's being summoned to Rome in 1481 by Pope Sixtus IV to paint frescoes in the Sistine Chapel, including narratives from the Life of Moses and the Temptation of Christ. Also working in Rome on this decorative cycle were Domenico Ghirlandaio, Pietro Perugino, Luca Signorelli, and Il Pinturicchio.

Botticelli returned to Florence immediately upon completion of the Sistine commission. At this time, "being of a sophistical turn of mind," he is reported by Vasari to have written a commentary on Dante and to have executed drawings for the *Inferno* that were adapted into engravings. Vasari's chronology is here compressed and confused. Botticelli evidently continued working on drawings associated with all three books of the *Divine Comedy* well into the 1490s; the *Inferno* illustrations are reflected, undoubtedly in simplified form, in the engraved illustrations that accompany the 1481 Landino Dante on exhibition here (Gardner Museum, Cat. 2). This sort of illustration, in which engravings were inserted into printed text, was both a technological and stylistic innovation. Both in its required emphasis on linear definition of figures, clearly and expressively communicating narrative in simple terms, and in the artist's prolonged devotion to the subject matter of Dante's profound religious morality play, the *Divine Comedy*, the impact of this extended project on Botticelli should not be underestimated. Vasari, who praises Botticelli's drawing and says that other artists sought examples of it after his death, tells us that Botticelli spent much time over these illustrations; he then notes that Botticelli executed a print of the *Triumph of Faith of Savonarola*, a more successful work (of which there is no trace). Vasari immediately follows this report with his discussion of Botticelli as a follower of Girolamo Savonarola. We know that Botticelli's brother Simone returned to Florence from Naples about 1494 and became an ardent disciple of Savonarola. Simone very likely influenced his brother to pay heed to the Dominican friar from Ferrara, who had become prior of the influential monastery of San Marco in Florence and effective ruler of Florence between 1494 and 1498. By 1497 Savonarola's influence had begun to wane and he was burnt at the stake for heresy in 1498. Indeed, Vasari asserts that Botticelli's adherence to the sect (becoming a Piagnone [whiner], as Savonarola's adherents were called) cost Botticelli his livelihood and reduced him to penury and illness. We now know that this politically opportune moral by Vasari is inaccurate, but there is little doubt that the character of Botticelli's art changed in this period.

Vasari concludes his biography with an extended list of Botticelli's works (confusedly also citing works by the minor artist Francesco Botticini, one of whose paintings [Cat. 5] is in the Gardner collection), ending with the *Calumny of Apelles*, now in the Uffizi, painted ca. 1494. In fact, Botticelli remained an esteemed painter and continued to receive lucrative commissions and to paint into the first decade of the sixteenth century, but in a style that had become increasingly archaistic in its adherence to stylistic conventions he had crystallized in the 1490s, although he was aware of current artistic innovations. Indeed, Botticelli was a member of the commission charged with determining where Michelangelo's sculpture of David should be sited in the city. Thus, at the same time Florence was witnessing the emergence of Michelangelo, Raphael, Fra Bartolommeo, and the mature accomplishments of Leonardo, among others, Botticelli created, for example, his late masterpiece *The Tragedy of Lucretia* (ca. 1502). That work, which is in the collection of the Gardner Museum and is included in this exhibition (Cat. 10), reflects Botticelli's knowledge both of classical art and architecture and of Flemish landscapes; it also alludes to the recent accomplishments of Domenico Ghirlandaio, while yet remaining true to Botticelli's own inimitable late stylistic vernacular. The *Lucretia* is one of a group of late, large paintings designed for the decoration of private residences that includes *The Story of Virginia* (ca. 1501–1504, Bergamo, Accademia Carrara), the dispersed series of *The Life and Miracles of San Zenobio* (1500–1505), and an unfinished *Adoration of the Magi* (Uffizi)—all executed in this late style characterized by the compulsive and impassioned expressiveness and gesturing of figures in simple, powerfully structured settings. By the time of his death in 1510, Botticelli's work was less contemporary to a society and culture that had, once again, moved on to different, humanistic concerns.

II. Patrons and Mentors

Vasari emphasizes the importance of the patronage of Lorenzo de' Medici (1449–1492) on the career of Botticelli in the opening sentence of his biography, and while the number of commissions received directly from Lorenzo is disputed, it is clear that Lorenzo's broader family and circle were responsible for several of the most famous of Botticelli's early and mature works. Lorenzo was the leading citizen of Florence after the death of his father, Piero, in 1469. The assassination of his brother Giuliano and the attempt on his own life in the Cathedral in Florence by an anti-Medicean conspiracy led by the Pazzi family in 1478 only strengthened his hold on the city. The 1470s was a period of cautious consolidation of political power for Lorenzo, but by the end of that decade there was little doubt about his authority over both internal affairs and foreign policy. While public opinion may not have been as supportive of Lorenzo as subsequent histories would claim (indeed, by the 1480s Lorenzo seems to have brooked little public statement of opposition, even within his extended family, without serious consequences on liberty and estate), everyone in Florence appreciated his influence, and the cultural leadership he provided was central to the artistic life of the city. Unquestionably Lorenzo was a tremendous and enlightened sponsor of the culture of Christian humanism in Florence. His breadth of interests—ranging from philosophy and classical literature to neo-Latin and vernacular poetry (he was himself an accomplished poet) to the theater and popular *feste* (both religious *sacre rappresentazioni* and carnevals featuring classical and more modern comedies) to new music to both ancient and contemporary fine arts—is justifiably legendary, and he surrounded himself with some of the greatest talents in these fields. These men exchanged ideas in the chambers and gardens of Lorenzo's palace in Florence and in country villas at Fiesole, Poggio a Caiano, Cafaggiolo, and Careggi (where there was an annual banquet in honor of Plato), and their influence extended to commissioned art works. As a celebrated example of the influence of this diverse cultural group, in Botticelli's *Primavera* the selection and processional depiction of the subject matter and the figures' attire derive not only from diverse sources in classical and Renaissance poetry but also from contemporary processional *feste*. Contemporary poetical conceits and ideals of womanly beauty and love, with actual Florentine female inspirations, are reflected in the painting's women.

Lorenzo was admirably educated for his position of leadership and was conscious of his place in a tradition of benefaction. His grandfather Cosimo, as head of the Medici faction that earlier dominated the city, a banking dynasty rather than aristocratic, had spent much money on the architectural enrichment of Florence (not without grumblings among jealous Florentines about the sprouting of golden balls [*palle*]—the Medici coat of arms—all over the city's buildings). While dressing and publicly comporting himself soberly, Cosimo nonetheless commissioned Michelozzo to build the grandiose palace in Florence that contributed to his temporary exile in the 1430s. He also surrounded himself with such artists and scholars as Donatello, whom he supported, Filippo Brunelleschi, Filippo Lippi, Fra Angelico, Poliziano, Platina, and Pico della Mirandola. A bibliophile, he assembled a library remarkable for its time that was virtually open to the public. He also was a patron who commissioned art works for various churches, convents, and monasteries, including the Dominican monastery of San Marco, for which he commissioned the decorations painted by Fra Angelico and his studio in the 1440s.

When Cosimo died in 1464, he was succeeded in an unofficial and private capacity by his mild, reserved, and well-liked son Piero, who with the assistance of his cultured and intelligent wife, Lucrezia Tournabuoni, ruled the city quietly, overcoming an attempt against his life by rival families, including the Pazzi, the Pitti, and the Strozzi, in 1466. Piero died in December 1469, leaving the leadership of Florence to his elder son Lorenzo, who had trained for it from his youth. Indeed, Lorenzo performed his first official state function at the age of five. By 1454 Lorenzo was entrusted to Gentile Becchi, who, though a priest (later Bishop of Arezzo), educated him in humanist readings, Latin, ancient literature, and poetry. In 1458, Lorenzo began attending lectures on rhetoric and poetics given by Cristoforo Landino at the University of Florence. (It was Landino who wrote the extended commentary for the 1481 edition of Dante's *Divine Comedy* [Cat. 2] that prints after Botticelli's early *Inferno* drawings serve to illustrate.) Under the guidance of Leon Battista Alberti, Lorenzo studied the ancient ruins of Rome. He studied music under the organist of the Cathedral, Antonio Squarcialupi, and learned to play several instruments. His father's infirmity led Lorenzo while still in his teens to undertake important diplomatic missions to Milan, Rome, and Naples, among other cities. For political reasons he was married in 1469 to Clarice Orsini, a daughter of one of the oldest and noblest Roman families, in spite of his longstanding love, memorialized in his poetry, for Lucrezia Donati of Florence.

In the 1470s Lorenzo gathered around him the cultural circle for which he would become famous. Over time it included the Christian philosopher and scholar of Plato, Marsilio Ficino; the poet, logician, and teacher of Aristotelian philosophy Angelo Poliziano; the poet Luigi Pulci; the aristocrat and classically-inspired author Giovanni Pico della Mirandola; and the bookseller Vespasiano da Bisticci. Botticelli, Domenico Ghirlandaio, and Filippino Lippi (the son of Filippo Lippi, who was trained by Botticelli) all worked for Lorenzo on the decoration of the villa of Spedaletto; Lorenzo's patronage also extended to Verrocchio and the Pollaiuolo brothers. In the last years of his life the "garden" of Lorenzo even embraced the young Michelangelo. That garden was a school that Lorenzo founded in a garden between the Palazzo Medici and the monastery San Marco, a school where artistic training was commingled with a broader education under the guidance of Bertoldo di Giovanni, an artist who himself had studied under Donatello. While Lorenzo supported artists and gave them access to his scholars and to his collections, there is no real evidence that he dealt with them on the same familiar terms that Cosimo had shared with his friend Donatello. Nonetheless, Lorenzo created a nurturing environment for their enrichment, both intellectual and financial, and his sophisticated commissions undoubtedly contributed to their own cultural advancement. The sort of idealization of form that we find in Botticelli's figures, in which classical perfection of feature and dreamy, introspective countenances convey a state of spiritual perfection, reflect the Platonic speculations of Lorenzo's circle. Similarly, the manipulation of perspective and the composition of his images of the Madonna and Child from the 1470s and 1480s, evident in the two Gardner paintings included in the exhibition (Cats. 1 and 3 [in which the composition curves inward]) through the gestures and movements of the figures, serve to guide the eye to the Infant, thus complementing the *desio* (the desire, longing) of the soul to embrace the Good and, traversing space, to unite itself with its source in God. These concerns also reflect, if not the direct study of Ficino, sympathy with current philosophical speculation.

Giuliano de' Medici, Lorenzo's younger brother (1452–1478), was an early patron of Botticelli, who executed a portrait of him in 1476–1477 (Washington, D.C., National Gallery of Art). Lorenzo's association with the artist began about the same time. His role in the commissioning of Botticelli's *Primavera* of 1478 has been disputed. That commission has sometimes been ascribed to Lorenzo's young cousin Lorenzo di Pierfrancesco de' Medici, but on the basis of later and possibly misleading inventories. Recent scholarship restores the likelihood that Lorenzo himself commissioned this painting together with the *Pallas and the Centaur* (1482, Florence, Uffizi). The origins of the *Birth of Venus* of 1482, however, remain obscure. While the number of Lorenzo's direct commissions appear limited, he seems to have ensured or at least approved the work Botticelli did for other prominent Florentines (for example, the Santa Maria Novella *Adoration of the Magi* for Guaspare del Lama), as well as approving Botticelli's work for the pope in the Sistine Chapel.

One particular commission of Botticelli must have met with Lorenzo's approval. In 1476 and 1477, members of a rival Florentine family, the Pazzi, conspired to overthrow the Medici, drawing several high-ranking politicians into their plot (including Girolamo Riario, lord of Imola and papal nephew, and Francesco Salviati, Archbishop of Pisa). Pope Sixtus IV evidently knew of the plot but hesitated at the killing of the brothers Lorenzo and Giuliano de' Medici. With the assistance of two corrupt clerics, the Medici brothers were attacked in the Cathedral on Sunday, April 26, 1478. The younger brother, the handsome, intelligent, and popular Giuliano, was brutally stabbed and killed, while, by quick action, Lorenzo escaped through the church. The population of Florence, shocked by the violence and sacrilege—and never particularly fond of the Pazzi—rallied overwhelmingly to Lorenzo and the Medici's cause. All of the Florentine conspirators, as well as Salviati, were apprehended and executed, the Pazzi family severely punished and prohibited from future involvement in Florentine affairs. Sandro Botticelli, no doubt with Lorenzo's consent, was commissioned by the city, for forty florins a figure, to paint images of the Pazzi traitors and their confederates on the walls of the Palazzo Vecchio. (It is a common inaccuracy in the literature of art history to site these on the facade of the Bargello.) Botticelli depicted them hanged by the neck, except for one conspirator, who had escaped and was painted hanging by his ankles. Lorenzo himself composed the verse-epitaphs that were painted beneath each figure.

In 1481, the Dominican friar Girolamo Savonarola, who was born in Ferrara in 1452, son and grandson of physicians to the Este ducal courts, arrived in Florence. Extremely austere in his manner and habits, he dedicated himself as a "knight for Christ," as he wrote to his father. He was appointed a lector at the monastery of San Marco and gave a Lenten sermon at San Lorenzo, the Medici church, the following spring. An awkward and unattractive preacher, Savonarola worked hard at improving his skills and through his urgent sincerity gradually built up a following. After five years he left Florence, returning at the invitation of Lorenzo, upon the urging of Pico della Mirandola. By 1491, he had become so popular that San Marco could not hold the congregation that came to hear him; for Lent that year he delivered his sermon in the Cathedral.

Savonarola was a zealot, prone to apocalyptic visions that appeared to him in conjunction with fasts and long, private meditations. He preached a return to the simplicity of the early Church, the burning of sodomites, and the repudiation of all fleshly attractions, luxuries, and idle pleasures of the world. Rejecting the reading of classical authors and philosophers (who, he reminded his congregation, were consigned to Hell), Savonarola urged the conformance of state law to the laws of God. Lorenzo tolerated the friar, who, although he gave final absolution to Lorenzo in 1492, was disdainful of the Medici. In one of the ironies of history, Lorenzo had expressed no objection to the appointment of the monk as prior of San Marco. Despite Lorenzo's position and major donations to the monastery from the Medici family, Savonarola refused to pay court to Florence's leading citizen, and indeed often attacked him from the pulpit, warning him about squandering public funds, urging him to repent, for God would punish him and his, and predicting that Lorenzo would go but he (Savonarola) would stay.

Lorenzo's death on April 8, 1492, at the age of forty-three, was followed by the brief, unpopular leadership of his son Piero. With the threat of an attack by the French prevented only by humiliating capitulations and Piero's own exile, public discontent against the Medici was unleashed and Savonarola's power grew. The French passed through Florence, the government was reformed, and Savonarola became, in effect, a leading power in the state. As is described in James Hankins' essay later in this catalogue, Savonarola's powerful apocalyptic sermons, his calls for Florence to repent, his frightening visions of the future, and his confidence in his own role as "watchman in the center of Italy" gripped large portions of the populace. Savonarola even demanded the death of those who would restore the Medici as he embarked on a sweeping program to reform the city state. Luxury items, art works, poetry, and all encouragements to vice, which he called vanities, were to be collected and destroyed. Gold and silver were to be removed from churches. The poetic art (which Savonarola himself had essayed earlier in his career) was described by the prior as the lowest of the sciences, and poets who "wallow" in their undertaking should rather flee their ignorance and "the unendurable stench of worthless glory," for sincerity of faith was more important than eloquence. Neither was knowledge of Greek or Hebrew desirable to a pious man since God had already given Saint Jerome to translate the Old and New Testaments into Latin.

Savonarola's commentaries on the visual arts are not well organized, and they are dispersed through his writings. Vasari tells us that Savonarola had held it was wrong to exhibit images of naked

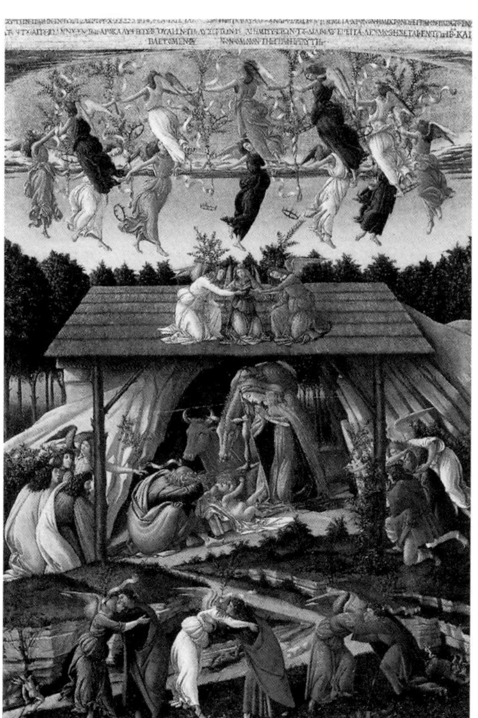

Figure 4. *The Mystical Nativity.* London, National Gallery.

men and women in houses where children could see them. He seems also to have been concerned that art follow theology and depict its subjects with decorum, complaining that contemporary images of the Madonna, Mary Magdalene, Saint Elizabeth, and Saint John should not be sumptuously dressed to resemble Florentine citizens (a distracting vanity for beholders), but rather should appear in costumes that reflect their poverty and simplicity. He sermonized against the vanity of invention and profane subjects, and he demeaned the stature of the visual arts with the observation that if art imitates nature, then certainly nature, the creation of God, is superior. There was little honor in deceiving the outward eye of men through art, he said; rather it is the inward eye to the spirit that should be cultivated. On the other hand, the prior seemingly did not object to the simple and pietistic representation of sacred subjects in conformance with scripture. As in his sermons, he seems to emphasize clear, direct, and simple imagery and presentation of narrative, decrying conscious eloquence and the vanity of elegance. In his *Sermons on Zacchariah*, Savonarola makes literary use of artists' studio practice. He draws an analogy between the intellect of God, in giving order to the universe, and the knowledge of fault and order of an artist in looking at an art work or examining the copy of his work by a pupil working from a print from the artist: "So too God in his concerns wished to make a print so that whoever falls away from that order is at fault, and will be punished thereafter." The analogy is interesting given Botticelli's work with printmakers at this date. Of course, Botticelli supplied drawings rather than prints, from which printmakers executed less successful adaptations in intaglio.

Savonarola encouraged Florentines of all ages to devout practices. Children were urged to process, singing hymns, through the streets of Florence, and the public was exhorted to fast. In the children's processions of February and March 1496, children carried olive branches, imagery that appears about five years later in Botticelli's *Mystical Nativity* (London, National Gallery, Fig. 4). Children also were encouraged to report on sumptuary infractions of their parents. The bonfire held at Carneval in 1497, the so-called "Bonfire of the Vanities," included expensive clothing, profane books (including writings of antiquity, poetry, and the works of Boccaccio), luxury items, game tables, portraits, jewelry, and costumes. A second bonfire was lit that year, and Vasari tells us that Baccia della Porta (Fra Bartolommeo) and Lorenzo di Credi contributed their own works to the flames.

Throughout 1495 and 1496, Savonarola's disobedience to the pope and his unwillingness to join in the Italian campaign against the French increasingly isolated him from Rome, which issued bans that he ignored. Successive poor harvests, outbreaks of plague, and war with Pisa further encouraged his enemies in Florence, previously a vocal minority. Although excommunicated in June 1497, Savonarola continued to preach, even as his support dwindled, until in his last public sermon in March 1498, without any moderation, he declared the Church a Satanic institution, promoting vice, and cried out, "I feel myself all burning, all inflamed with the spirit of the Lord." The words were prophetic. After an aborted ordeal by fire in April 1498, riots broke out, Savonarola was arrested in his library, tortured into a confession, tortured again, convicted of heresy and schism, and finally hanged by chains from a scaffold and burned on May 23. Even after this series of events, however, he remained a fixture of the Florentine psyche. As the year 1500 approached and amidst economic and social unrest and outbreaks of plague, there was a recovery of interest in some quarters in the late prior. His name became tied in the Florentine imagination not only with religious fanaticism but also, more enduringly, with radical republican reform.

We know that Botticelli's brother Simone, the della Robbia family, the architect Cronaca, the artist Lorenzo di Credi, and Giorgio Antonio Vespucci—all close to Botticelli—were followers of Savonarola. That Botticelli was responsive to—or at least was familiar with the teachings of—Savonarola is evident from such paintings as London's *Mystical Nativity* and Harvard's *Mystical Crucifixion* (Cat. 8), an apocalyptic image painted ca. 1500 that shows the salvation of a repentant Florence as foretold in Savonarola's sermons or possibly the treatise of a follower. Even earlier, Harvard's sober, extremely simple devotional image of *Christ the Redeemer* from the Studio of Botticelli, also on exhibition (Cat. 4), probably dating to the early 1490s, anticipates the intense and unelaborated piety of the sort that Savonarola preached. Together with the directness of expression and gesture and the passionate tone of these pictures, there is an abjuration of sumptuous attire in these paintings that is consonant with Savonarola's attitude toward decorum, though a certain richness begins to re-emerge in the gold trim of the Virgin's robe in the *Virgin and Child with Saint John the Baptist* (ca. 1500, Boston, Museum of Fine Arts, Cat. 9), and fully in the later and more secular and politically nuanced *Tragedy of Lucretia*.

The first indications of a revision in Botticelli's late style emerged as early as ca. 1481 in his designs for the *Inferno* and developed in the further designs for the *Divine Comedy* that he drew throughout the 1490s to ca. 1501. Dante's epic poem of the journey of the human soul through its witness of sin and repentance to redemption—familiar to any educated Florentine—was the perfect vehicle for the transformation of Botticelli's art. The work was the extended subject of much contemplation by Botticelli, who knew the Medicean Dante scholar Landino (see Cat. 2). The spiritual concerns of the text were also the concerns of Florence in the 1490s. The new medium of text illustration and intaglio prints required simple, legible narrative with powerful gesture and clear content, emphasizing contour line, the figures thus appearing flat. Botticelli's later drawings, preserved in the Vatican and Berlin, are far more compositionally complex and artistically compelling than the prints done, as Vasari notes, "in a bad manner because the cutting was badly done." The prints from the 1480s are more literal to the text, compressing several scenes; they also contain the most modelled and idealized figures. The figures move with increasing directness and passionate gestures in the later works. This evolution is also evident in a comparison of the illustrational prints drawn after the early *Inferno* designs (Cat. 2) with the large *Assumption* from the Museum of Fine Arts, Boston (Cat. 7), an engraving after a design by Botticelli dating to ca. 1495–1500, which is also included in the exhibition.

Botticelli's works are thus testimony not only to his evolving artistic ambitions but also to an understanding of himself and his society that was tempered in the crucible of intellectual and spiritual crisis. As Proust observed, "Thanks to art, instead of seeing one world only, our own, we see that world multiply itself and we have at our disposal as many worlds as there are original artists . . . worlds which, centuries after the extinction of the fire from which their light first emanated . . . send us still each one its special radiance."

From the New Athens to the New Jerusalem: Florence Between Lorenzo de' Medici and Savonarola

James Hankins

What has Athens to do with Jerusalem?
—Tertullian

During the night of April 5, 1492, the lantern of the great cupola of Santa Maria del Fiore, the cathedral church of Florence, was struck by lightning, causing great damage. It was a portentous and terrifying event for a superstitious age, made all the more so by a coincidence of events. During the storm the famous preacher Girolamo Savonarola had had a vision, causing words to break spontaneously from his lips: "Ecce gladius Domini super terram, cito et velociter" ("Behold, the sword of the Lord comes swiftly and soon upon the earth"). He had seen these words emblazoned on a sword held high in the heavens over Florence. Flights of angels were descending, offering to every mortal a white robe and a red cross. Some accepted the robes, others did not. Then the divine hand that held the sword rained down fire and lightning, plague, war, famine, and destruction upon the city. On the morning of the sixth, Savonarola explained the meaning of the vision in a sermon to the terrified Florentines. The Lord God was coming at last to chastise the lukewarm, the sinners, and the corrupt of the earth. Unless Florence repented and reformed herself, she would be consumed by fire and sword.

That same morning the ruler of Florence, Lorenzo de' Medici, lay dying a few miles away in his villa at Careggi. When he heard the news that a thunderbolt had struck the cathedral, he took it, according to a contemporary diarist, as a portent of his own death. Two days later he did indeed die, having received the blessing of Savonarola. Untrustworthy sources later whispered that Savonarola had in fact refused Lorenzo absolution when that prince found himself unable to perform the penance the preacher had set him: to restore free government to the Florentines.

It is understandable that the dramatic events of April 1492 should appear to historians to form a watershed in the story of Florence and the Renaissance. It was a year of great events. In April, the Christian rulers of Spain captured the Moorish kingdom of Granada, bringing an end to seven centuries of Muslim power in the Iberian peninsula; in the same year they sought to purify Christianity in their realms by expelling the Jews from Spain. In August Alexander VI, the most worldly and corrupt of the Renaissance popes, was elevated to the See of Peter. Late in the year, Europe began hearing rumors of new lands to the west discovered by a Genoese adventurer named Christopher Columbus. In Italy, the death of Lorenzo and the succession to power of his feckless son Piero soon undermined the balance of power among the states of that peninsula. By 1494 the sixty-year dominance of the Medici in Florentine politics was at an end; the King of France, Charles VIII, emboldened by Italian disunity, had marched through Italy from the Alps to Naples; and Florence was in the grip of both a political revolution and an extraordinary religious awakening that would reverberate in Tuscany for half a century. The animating spirit of both the revolution and the spiritual awakening was the Dominican friar Girolamo Savonarola, who became the virtual ruler of Florence from late in 1494 until the early months of 1498.

The temptation to see the years from 1492 to 1494 as a cusp joining distinct eras of Florentine history is made stronger by the contrast between the two personalities that dominated Florence in the periods before and after. Indeed, it is difficult to imagine two men more different than Lorenzo de' Medici (1449–1492) and his near-contemporary, Girolamo Savonarola (1452–1498). Lorenzo was the grandson of Cosimo de' Medici (1389–1464), the banker and statesman who in 1434 had established the ascendancy of his family in Florentine politics. Brilliant, well educated, immensely wealthy and powerful, Lorenzo was a bundle of contradictions as puzzling to modern historians as to his contemporaries. He could throw himself with zest into civic festivities, yet he loved the peace of country life and the beauty of nature. He could write deeply-felt religious poetry and refined love lyrics but also bawdy and satire. He was a voluptuary and a cynic yet he devoted himself and his wealth to the highest cultural and religious enterprises. Abroad he was an effective force for peace among the Italian states, while at home he played a rough and often corrupt game of machine politics. A loving father and a generous friend, he could react with sudden cruelty when his authority was challenged. In the historian Guicciardini's words, he was "the best and most agreeable of tyrants."

Lorenzo inherited the leadership of the Medici party at the age of twenty, upon the death of his father Piero, but his youth caused misgivings among the party's elders. Making a virtue of what the elders saw as a liability, he and his brother, Giuliano, turned youth, love, beauty, and the rebirth of culture into the themes of Florentine civic life. Under their encouragement, Florentines sang and danced and feasted and played and adorned themselves as never before, in bursts of elegant festivity that historians have ever after seen as the purest expressions of the Florentine Renaissance. Lorenzo sought to elevate these festivals to the status of high art, hiring famous artists (including Botticelli and Andrea del Verrocchio) to design the costumes and decorations, and himself composing verses to be sung by the participants. The spirit of these festivals is caught perfectly by Lorenzo's verses *The Triumph of Bacchus and Ariadne* with the famous refrain,

Quant' é bella giovanezza	[How lovely now is youth's allure,
Che si fugge tuttavia!	Yet how quickly shall it flee!
Chi vuole esser lieta sia:	Let who would be happy, be:
Di doman non c'é certezza.	From tomorrow nothing's sure.]

But Lorenzo's Renaissance was more than pageantry and festival. Behind the public magnificence was a serious program of cultural renewal. Like all such programs in that age, it was breathtakingly ambitious. Lorenzo's goal was nothing less than to make Florence the heir to Athens and Rome, to make her the capital of the third great civilization of the Western world. Lorenzo believed, as had many Italians from the time of Petrarch, that cultural greatness could be achieved only by first sitting at the feet of the poets, artists, philosophers, and statesmen of Greco-Roman antiquity. So setting out to build his New Athens (as Angelo Poliziano called it), Lorenzo followed a careful plan to recover the wisdom, arts, and virtues of the ancient world. To that end he refounded the University of Florence in 1473, giving to ancient philosophy and literature an autonomy and prominence in the curriculum they had never before possessed. He brought Italy's greatest teachers to Florence to teach the classics to Florentine youth. Platonism, the most sublime of the ancient philosophical traditions, was revived through the efforts of Lorenzo's protégé, Marsilio Ficino. Inspired by stories about the ancient royal library of Alexandria, Lorenzo built the greatest library in Italy, in which the literary heritage of Greco-Roman antiquity was assembled for the use of scholars. Finally, he also created in the Medici palace itself and in the nearby monastery of San Marco the most brilliant collection of classical antiquities to be found anywhere outside Rome itself. Scholars and artists came there from all over Europe to increase their understanding of the glorious past. Florence overflowed with the most dazzling assemblage of literary, artistic, and scholarly talent the Quattrocento could show.

But the goal of Lorenzo and his circle was never mere imitation of past glories. Though inspired by the past, the New Athens had its own language, its own religious wisdom, its own ideals of love and courtliness. Lorenzo's aim, like Dante's and Alberti's before him, was to transfer the clarity and beauty of the ancient languages to Tuscan. Tuscan would become the third great classical language. The Florentine literary tradition would be ennobled and refined, made worthy of an imperial people. Through the study of ancient philosophy, Tuscan artists and writers would tap the esoteric wisdom thought to be concealed in the greatest ancient poetry and art. A delicate balance would be struck between the profundity and daemonic art of the ancients and the liveliness and courtly grace of the moderns. The artists, architects, philosophers, and writers of the 1470s and 1480s—preeminently Botticelli, Verrocchio, Ficino, Poliziano, Antonio Pollaiuolo, Giuliano da San Gallo, Pico della Mirandola, and Lorenzo himself—all in their own ways aimed at this elegant harmony of ancient and modern values.

It is too much to say that the peculiarly Laurentian synthesis of classical and Tuscan sprang entirely from the brain of Lorenzo himself or was entirely dependent on his patronage. Scholars nowadays rightly resist the temptation to explain cultural history in terms of dominant personalities. Yet it is difficult to escape the conviction that Savonarola's rise to power after the death of Lorenzo signaled a major shift in Florentine cultural values. As we shall see, there are continuities as well as contrasts between the Laurentian and Savonarolan periods, but at first sight it is the contrasts that leap to the eye.

To read through the sermons of Savonarola from the later 1490s is to see the Laurentian period with new eyes. For Savonarola and his followers (called the *Piagnoni*, or the Weepers), the Medici regime had been nothing but a thinly veiled tyranny that had brought about the moral enslavement of the Florentines. Tyrants were by nature actuated by the lowest motives, and their rule inevitably corrupted the morals of their subjects, leading to the triumph of rapacity, lust, and greed. Lorenzo's patronage of arts and letters was vitiated by disordered values and worldly priorities. Lorenzo had corrupted religion by surrounding himself with fashionable preachers who had done nothing to arrest moral decline. The revival of Platonism that had taken place under his aegis threatened to undermine the sound theological traditions of the Church. He had weakened the authority of Christianity by cooperating with a corrupt system of church government. Lorenzo's grandfather, Cosimo, had famously stated that a state could not be governed with paternosters; Savonarola declared, to the contrary, that no state could flourish unless it were founded on firm religious principles.

The man who uttered these condemnations of the Medici regime had a background strikingly different from Lorenzo's. He was born in 1452 in Ferrara to a family of physicians and merchants closely connected with the ducal court of the d'Este. After a course of humanistic studies, which failed to strike deep roots in his mind, Savonarola began to study medicine with a view toward emulating the brilliant career of his grandfather, Michele Savonarola, court physician to the d'Este. But the young man was already coming to be possessed by that dark vision of the corruption of the world and its need for reformation that would later drive him to seek power and martyrdom. He soon abandoned medicine for theology and, against the will of his parents, decided in 1475 to become a Dominican friar. The Dominicans, sensing Savonarola's intelligence and commitment, prepared him to become a preacher. In 1482 he became a theology teacher at the monastery of San Marco in Florence, later the center of his religious awakening. He remained in Florence for five years, making, it seems, little impression on the religious life of the city.

In 1490 Savonarola was brought back to Florence by Lorenzo de' Medici himself, at the instance of the philosopher Giovanni Pico della Mirandola, one of Lorenzo's intimates. This time Savonarola's preaching had an entirely different effect. From the beginning, Savonarola cloaked his message in the mantle of prophecy. In sermon after sermon he trained his fire on the moral failings of the Florentines, the vices of the clergy and the papal court, the need for reformation, and the tribulations that awaited Florentines if they did not amend their lives. His manner, too, was new. Contemporaries mentioned his incandescent eyes, his deep and electrifying voice, his passionate sincerity, his magnetism. His audiences increased dramatically, numbering at their height (according to contemporaries) as many as thirteen to fourteen thousand—a remarkable number in a city of at most 60,000 people. In 1491 he was elected Prior of San Marco, and the monastery soon became the center of Florentine religious life, attracting hundreds of converts. In due course the convent of San Marco separated itself from the Lombard Congregation of Dominicans, to which it had hitherto belonged, and became the mother house of its own reformed congregation, with Savonarola as its vicar general. Fra Girolamo had taken his place among the most influential clerics in Italy.

In 1494 affairs took a dramatic turn. The military advance of the French king, Charles VIII, along with political turmoil in Florence itself, made it appear that the dire prophecies Savonarola had so often uttered were about to be fulfilled. The immediate threat of a sack by the French army, and the flight of Lorenzo's son Piero on November 9, gave Savonarola the leverage he needed to impose his will on the terrified city. As his voice from the pulpit of Santa Maria del Fiore seemed the one effective source of authority amid the terror and chaos, the city's political elite turned to him for guidance. Savonarola's diplomatic skills proved effective in preventing a sack of the city, and his calls for Christian forbearance were credited with averting a bloodbath in the city between Medici partisans and their enemies. Real political power and boundless prestige were suddenly his. Emboldened, Savonarola prepared to build the New Jerusalem of which he had so long dreamed.

Clearly, Savonarola owed his newfound power to more than his charisma as a preacher and his good fortune as a prophet. He was also able to exploit generations of pent-up hostility to Medicean rule. Savonarola was clever enough to give the shortcomings of the Medici regime a powerful religious interpretation, directing the general animus against the Medici into his desired channels of political and moral reform. The Medici, he declared, had brought Florence to the brink of destruction by suppressing her ancient republican traditions of self-rule and participation in civic life. Public virtue could not flourish when all decisions had to be referred to a few political bosses. Political freedom and broad participation in government, Savonarola believed, were only possible in the context of moral reform. True liberty was holy liberty, *santa libertà*. Florence needed a new constitution that would give power back to the people and restore community. Only then would the natural goodness of ordinary Christian people succeed in purifying politics. Only then would Florence fulfill her destiny as an elect nation that would lead the rest of Christendom into the millennium.

These flattering promises drew on centuries of Florentine political mythology in which the City of the Lilies had figured as the daughter and heir to Rome, as a city specially beloved of God, destined to be the New Jerusalem. The Florentines suddenly found themselves transformed from a race doomed to perdition into a Chosen People. This, unsurprisingly, they found an attractive change of condition. Savonarola was able to begin his program of political and moral reform with a vigorous burst of public enthusiasm. The constitution was reformed so as to make Florentine politics seem more open and populist. A wave of moral legislation was passed by the Signoria, Florence's governing body, with the aim of creating a just and godly society. Taverns were shut; public gambling and blasphemy were outlawed; sodomy, that famous Florentine vice, was brutally repressed; and conspicuous consumption, especially spending on women's clothes, was tightly regulated. Artistic and literary works that aroused lust were to be destroyed. Horse races, jousts, and public festivities, including Carnival, were suppressed or transformed into religious observances. Penalties for lawbreaking were made harsher, enforcement more strict. There were calls to expel the city's prostitutes and Jews. Anyone who criticized Fra Girolamo was severely punished, while good citizens were admonished to live in all simplicity and godliness, preparing for the day of the Lord.

It was in this spirit that Savonarola organized the famous "Bonfire of the Vanities" for February 7, 1497, a day that before Savonarola's rise to power would have been celebrated with licentious gaiety as Mardi Gras. Savonarola observed the day in quite a different manner. He caused to be erected in the Piazza de' Signori a wooden pyramid fitted with steps, on which were arrayed all the "anathemata" that Savonarola's youthful followers had been able to collect: women's wigs and cosmetics, perfumes, looking glasses, lascivious books and paintings, dice and playing cards, lutes and love potions. Processions of boys then marched to the square singing hymns in praise of Jesus and in condemnation of Carnival. Fire was set to the wooden pyramid while bells rang, children sang, and the *pifferi* of the Signoria played their cornetti and sackbuts, to the joy (as a sympathetic source wrote) of the entire populace.

Reports soon began to circulate abroad about the remarkable transformation that seemed to have swept through Florence. Most remarkable—miraculous, said some—was the change in the behavior of Florentine youth. Florence's young men had long been notorious for being vicious and wild: throwing stones at passers-by, shouting insults at women and clerics, shaking down defenceless foreign visitors. Foreigners and city officials had complained about the situation for more than a century. Savonarola responded to the problem by creating a great youth confraternity that enrolled all the youth of the city, organized by region and age. Pious young men and women of high social station were recruited as leaders. Soon Florentine children and adolescents found themselves engaged in charitable works, visiting widows and the sick, admonishing their wayward elders, hounding prostitutes from the streets, and jamming themselves into church every day to hear Savonarola preach. It was Savonarola's greatest triumph—a sure sign, many said, that his reformation had the approval of God. Others, less well disposed, said that Fra Girolamo had inaugurated a dictatorship of virtue led by fanatical infants.

Less well known than the moral reforms associated with Savonarola are the steps he took to improve Florence's system of social welfare. Fra Girolamo blamed the Medici for wasting money on extravagances like festivals and the university while allowing the poor to sink into misery and the gap between rich and poor to widen. Savonarola insisted that a true Christian polity could not exist where large segments of the population lived like animals from hand to mouth. It was incumbent on the government and the rich, he said, to provide alms and jobs for the poor. Savonarola saw to it that public and private funds were spent on confraternities and on hospitals devoted to the care of the sick and indigent. He organized processions of children to collect money for his causes. Churches were urged to melt down their gold and silver ornaments to feed the poor. Dowries were provided for needy young women so that they might not fall into prostitution. Most important in his eyes was the organization of a *Monte di Pietà*, a public fund for lending money to the poor that would help them avoid the sin of usury—and evade the clutches of Jewish moneylenders. The *Monte di Pietà* also had the benefit, from the Piagnoni point of view, of making it easier to eject the Jews from God's chosen city. Legislation to that effect was passed on December 28, 1495.

But it is difficult for any state to breathe the air of Christian purity forever. Purist communities have sometimes maintained their moral fervor for decades, as happened in Calvinist Geneva and Puritan Boston. In Florence's case, the Savonarolan movement was able to stay in power for fewer than four years. Even before he was imprisoned in April of 1498, Savonarola's fortunes had risen and fallen numerous times. He probably never had a majority of the populace firmly on his side, and his position of unofficial leadership depended on a delicate system of internal and foreign alliances. He had been embroiled continually in battles of the pulpit and of the press with critics both lay and religious. His political enemies, the Arrabiati (or Angry Ones), worked tirelessly for his destruction. He had to contend with the implacable hostility of Pope Alexander VI, who silenced him, demoted him, and ultimately excommunicated him. It was the pope's added threat of interdict, which would have devastated Florentine trade, combined with the collapse of the friar's foreign alliances, that ultimately lost Savonarola the support of the Signoria and put an end to his career.

Once the decline began, the fall came with remarkable speed. In April of 1498 there occurred the slightly comic episode (to more secular eyes) of the "trial by fire." A Franciscan opponent, Fra Francesco di Puglia, challenged Savonarola's spokesman, Fra Domenico da Pescia, to a trial by fire to test the truth of Savonarola's teachings and the validity of his excommunication. With the support of the Signoria, this absurd and barbaric spectacle was allowed to take place on April 7. An enormous fire pit was constructed in the Piazza de' Signori through which the holy champions were to carry the Host, if God so willed, unscathed. In effect, Savonarola was expected to perform a miracle to prove his innocence and the truth of his teachings. On the day of the trial, however, the respective parties managed to prolong the proceedings with technical disputes until a convenient thunderstorm put an end to the embarrassing situation. Both sides declared victory.

But the populace had been disappointed of their miracle, and public sentiment veered suddenly and viciously against the Frate. On the next day, Palm Sunday, San Marco was attacked by a violent mob. After a siege of some hours during which hundreds were killed or maimed, Savonarola surrendered himself with two of his companions to the officers of the Signoria. He was imprisoned in the palace of the Signori (see Fig. 5). After many days of barbaric torture on the *strappado*, which left the Friar a twisted cripple, a confession was produced in which, it was alleged, Savonarola had admitted that his prophecies and his mission had all been lies and impostures. At this point the pope, wishing to be in on the kill, sent an apostolic commission to try the Friar for heresy. The sentence of heresy having been duly passed, on the following day, May 23, Savonarola and his two followers were hanged and their bodies burned before the palace of the Signori. By order of the Signoria, the ashes of the three martyrs were swept up and strewn in the Arno, lest they be collected as relics by the pious.

Historians have long been at pains to understand how a movement such as Savonarola's could have taken root in a city like Florence, the heart of the Italian Renaissance. How could a population so well educated, sophisticated, and cosmopolitan as Florence's have bred what appears to some

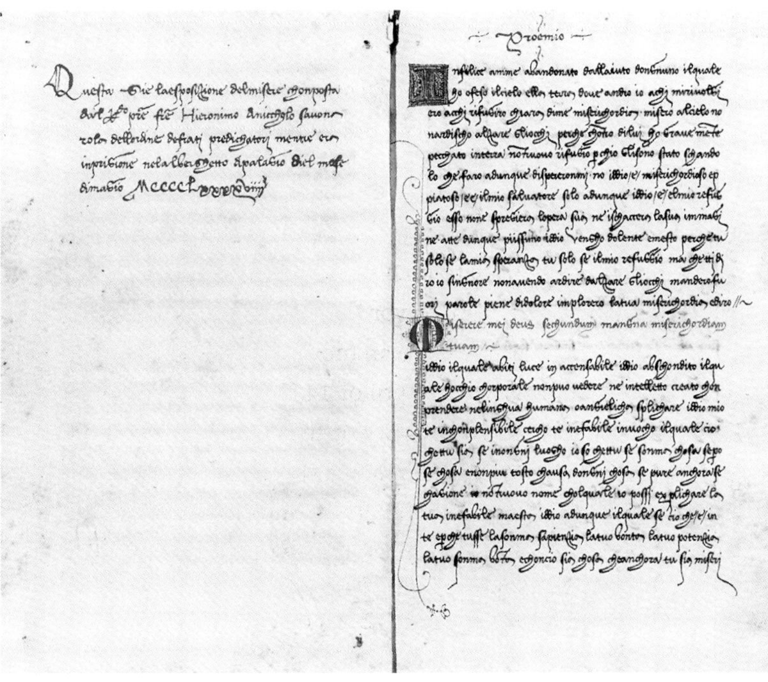

Figure 5. Girolamo Savonarola, *Più opere di fragirolamo di ferara*. Italian manuscript by unknown hand, ca. 1498–1499. The text on the left describes Savonarola's execution in 1498. MS Ital. 102, Houghton Library, Harvard University.

modern eyes a kind of narrow religious fundamentalism? An older generation of historians saved the phenomena by speaking of a "medieval" reaction to the "paganism" of the Renaissance, or of Savonarola as a "forerunner" of the Reformation. It was long assumed that Fra Girolamo and his Piagnone movement represented a populist reaction to the elitism of the Medici party, a struggle of "low culture" against "high culture," a protest against the enslavement of genuine Christianity to corrupt powers of Church and State.

Such interpretations are less easy for historians to accept today. The sharp ideological contrasts once thought to distinguish Savonarola from the Medici have blurred in light of a more critical scrutiny of contemporary sources. Indeed, Professor Lorenzo Polizzotto has recently argued that Savonarola in the early 1490s was the willing instrument of a project to strengthen the Medici's influence within the Tuscan church. Careful research, moreover, has shown that the class distinctions formerly supposed to have divided the Mediceans and the Piagnoni simply did not exist. Members of the political elite in Florence were, if anything, more likely than not to endorse Savonarola's reforms. Indeed, the most extraordinary thing about the Savonarolans was the number of former members of Lorenzo de' Medici's entourage they enrolled in their ranks. Angelo Poliziano, the greatest scholar-poet of the Renaissance and the chief luminary of Lorenzo's court, died in the Dominican habit; so did Giovanni Pico della Mirandola, the outstanding philosopher of Medicean Florence and Lorenzo's protégé. Both had come strongly under Savonarola's influence before their deaths. Marsilio Ficino, the Platonic philosopher and Medici guru, ended up hostile to Savonarola, but many in his circle, including the humanist scholars Giorgio Antonio Vespucci and Zanobi Acciaiuoli, the philosopher Giovanni Nesi, and the poet Girolamo Benivieni, became disciples of the Frate. Indeed, one of Ficino's favorite pupils, Francesco Valori, became the most prominent political leader of the Piagnoni. Artists, too, who had formerly worked for the Medici—most famously Michelangelo, Botticelli, and Lorenzo di Credi—became adherents and sympathizers of Savonarola.

The ease with which Mediceans became Savonarolans reminds us that, for all the striking contrasts between the age of the Medici and the age of Savonarola, there were also real continuities. Though in certain respects it was a reaction against Renaissance culture, the Savonarolan reform was also, in other respects, a true expression of the Renaissance. If one considers the case of Marsilio Ficino, for example, it becomes clear (as Donald Weinstein observed in *Savonarola and Florence: Prophecy and Patriotism in the Renaissance*) that Ficino's hostility to Savonarola was that of a rival Christian reformer, not that of a crypto-pagan critic. Ficino, too, had claimed to be a prophet of religious renewal. He, too, had gathered many members of Lorenzo's circle around him, exciting them with the prospect of reform. Ficino's Platonic Renaissance was in part a religious movement that aimed to strengthen

Christian theology and apologetics, educate the clergy, reform wayward youth, and combat the impious skepticism of their elders. He, too, emphasized an inward reform of spirit that tended to devalue the role of what Martin Luther would later call "works." He, too, had supported Lorenzo's challenge to the authority of the pope after the Pazzi conspiracy of 1478. Savonarola's reform movement was more radical, more popular, and infinitely more effective than Ficino's, but it was not fundamentally different.

Nor is the contrast between Savonarola's reform and humanist culture as great as has been imagined. Savonarola always wished to be taken for a man of learning, but he had little use for classical philology, and he shared the view of Saint Antoninus of Florence that the age's devotion to classical culture was exaggerated and potentially harmful as challenging the integrity of Christian culture. At the same time, he did not oppose the study of appropriate classical literature for the young. Indeed, Savonarola could not but have approved some of the aims of the humanist movement. Humanist educators of the Quattrocento believed fervently that the study of classical literature would improve the moral virtue and citizenship of their pupils. The noble Greeks and Romans were the best possible inspiration for a citizen body that needed above all to learn to set the public good above private interest. The classics would teach the young to value free participation in public life and detest tyranny. Most humanist educators indignantly rejected the suggestion that reading Greco-Roman authors would lead students to embrace pagan values. On this point Savonarola had a few reservations—the Bible, he believed, gave the best possible lessons in citizenship—but with the larger humanist aims of nourishing public virtue and resisting tyranny he had nothing but sympathy.

Finally, one may find in the very ambition of Savonarola's reform some similarities to Lorenzo's plans for Florence. The New Athens did, after all, have something to do with the New Jerusalem. The extraordinary cultural ambition, the boundless belief in the possibilities of human nature, the powerful will to renew corrupted communities in accordance with an idealized past—all these themes were highly characteristic of the Laurentian period and of the Renaissance in general. If Lorenzo strove to make Tuscan civilization the third great classical civilization of the West, Poliziano worked to create a great encyclopedia embracing all human knowledge. Ficino wanted to bring in a millennium in which the shattered unity of piety and wisdom would be restored for the first time since antiquity. Pico della Mirandola aimed to build a grand systematic theology that would bring together the religious wisdom of all the ages—pagan and Christian, Muslim and Jewish—with a view to putting an end, once and for all, to religious strife. These were not small ambitions. Nor were they mere toys of the imagination built by otherworldly dreamers. They were serious programs for research and action. In this context, Savonarola's ambition to transform Florence into a New Jerusalem, to make Florence into a true Christian community, assumes a new complexion. It was not, in the end, fundamentally different from all those other great Renaissance projects to transform the world, human nature, and human society. It was merely more successful.

Alessandro Filipepi, Called Botticelli

Laurence Kanter

Few artists from any period or any culture have enjoyed the posthumous fame and admiration that the world has accorded to Sandro Botticelli. For a large part of the public his name has become a password summoning to mind virtually the complete civilization of the Florentine Renaissance, an age dominated by such larger-than-life personalities as Lorenzo the Magnificent, Girolamo Savonarola, and Leonardo da Vinci. It is now almost impossible to imagine this era peopled by any but the languorous, elegant youths and benevolently wise elders of Botticelli's painted histories, clothed in anything but the garments of his Virgins and goddesses, unfolding anywhere but in the manicured landscapes of his Nativities and Epiphanies. Images like Botticelli's *Birth of Venus* are as universally recognized, and appreciated, as the *Mona Lisa* or any self-portrait by Rembrandt or Van Gogh. But it is salutary to remember that Botticelli was not always the object of popular veneration that he is today. Sufficient evidence survives to suggest that during his lifetime he was as well respected as any of his fellow craftsmen in Florence, but not necessarily more so. Some sources even imply that his old age was difficult, perhaps destitute, and that but for the generosity of a pension provided by his early patrons, Botticelli would have died of starvation, a forgotten man.

After his death in 1510, Botticelli seems chiefly to have been remembered in stories and anecdotes—for the most part anecdotes concerned with his reckless sense of humor—that were current among the painters' studios of Florence. These stories were codified and recorded, along with a short list of his works, in Giorgio Vasari's biography of the artist included in the *Lives of the Most Eminent Painters, Sculptors and Architects*, first published in 1550 and then slightly amplified in an edition of 1568. According to Vasari, Botticelli was "whimsical and eccentric," an artist of great promise and potential who "lived without due care." Among his other follies was too intense an interest in Dante, an obsession over which "he wasted much time" and that "caused infinite disorder in his affairs." Vasari was as much a raconteur and art critic as a disciplined historian. He did not know Botticelli personally; many of his remarks about the artist's personality were either taken from hearsay or assumed from interpreting his paintings. Nevertheless, the sketchy portrait of the artist that Vasari presented in his *Lives* remained Botticelli's official and authoritative biography for well over three hundred years.

The eclipse of Botticelli's reputation that began late in his own lifetime endured through the sixteenth, seventeenth, and eighteenth centuries, a period during which nearly everything painted earlier than Raphael was neglected—at best forgotten, at worst discarded as useless or outdated. One of Botticelli's supreme masterpieces, the *Adoration of the Magi* (Fig. 3) now in the Uffizi, was purchased sometime during that period by the Medici grand dukes of Tuscany, not because they esteemed the painter or valued its qualities as a work of art, but rather because it contains portraits of three of their forebears: Cosimo the Elder, Giuliano, and Giovanni de' Medici. Although Vasari described this painting in detail, praising it as one of Botticelli's finest ("it is indeed a most admirable work: the composition, the design, and the coloring are so beautiful that every artist who examines it is astonished"), it was mislabeled as having been painted by Domenico Ghirlandaio until 1845, when its true authorship was finally recognized. Similar stories could be recounted for any number of other pictures by Botticelli now classed among the canonical masterpieces of Western painting. The large *Pallas and the Centaur*, also now in the Uffizi, was discovered in 1895 hanging in the Palazzo Pitti, where it had presumably hung since shortly after it was painted. Isabella Stewart Gardner's *Madonna of the Eucharist* (Cat. 1), one of the most widely admired of all Botticelli's Madonna and Child compositions, was identified only in 1892, belonging (as it must have done since at least the seventeenth century) to the Princes Chigi in Rome, while the *Story of Virginia* now in Bergamo—a pendant to the Gardner *Tragedy of Lucretia* (Cat. 10)—was found perhaps not more than a quarter century earlier in a Roman pawn shop.

The first half of the nineteenth century saw a general revival of interest in early Italian painting and the formation of many of the great private and public collections in Germany, France, and Great Britain. Botticelli's reputation, however, did not benefit more than incidentally from the initial phases of this rediscovery. At a time when collectors and scholars were attracted to the spirituality, purity, and supposed naïveté of Italian "Primitives" (as pre-sixteenth-century panel paintings were and still are sometimes called), Botticelli could not discard the stigma, assigned to him by Vasari, of being whimsical and eccentric—"an extravagant and bizarre mind" (*cervello stravagante e bizzarro*), as he was described in a dictionary of painters published in 1719. As late as 1864, the panoramic and in some respects still unsuperseded *New History of Painting in Italy* written by J. A. Crowe and G. B. Cavalcaselle found it difficult to justify even the relative importance assigned to Botticelli by Vasari. Too many of his works, the authors thought, were too coarsely executed or too repetitive to betray the hand and mind of a truly great artist. For Crowe and Cavalcaselle, as for most art critics and historians in mid-Victorian Europe, the apogee of Italian painting at the end of the fifteenth century, one of its moments of greatest glory, was represented not by the restless and disquieting poetry of Botticelli but by the decorous monumentality and pure-minded solemnity of Domenico Ghirlandaio, whose genius they compared only to Giotto's and Michelangelo's.

A change in Botticelli's critical fortunes may first be detected in England in 1870, in a brief essay submitted to the *Fortnightly Review* by Walter Pater. Proceeding from the admission that Botticelli was a "secondary painter" and therefore perhaps not "a proper subject for general criticism," Pater nonetheless sought to describe and explain "the peculiar quality of pleasure which his work has the property of exciting in us, and which we cannot get elsewhere." Four years later, the great English art critic John Ruskin officially launched the cult of Botticelli, which thrives undiminished to this day, calling the artist "the greatest of all [Florentine] masters" and his paintings "alike in pure manual skill and pure mental passion . . . beyond all other work in Italy." Ruskin deliberately taunted his Victorian contemporaries and predecessors by addressing their conservative prejudices: "Ghirlandajo is a goldsmith selling plated goods; Botticelli's is pure gold tried in the fire, and engraved as Bezaleel and Aholiab engraved. . . . He is in one the most learned theologian, the most perfect artist, and the most kind gentleman whom Florence produced." Such extravagant and romantic praise naturally appealed to poets and painters like Dante Gabriel Rossetti and Edward Burne-Jones, as well as to the highly and self-consciously cultivated public that supported their work. By the 1880s, Botticelli's name was so commonly invoked in Britain as a yardstick of taste and quality that it could be lampooned in popular theater. One of the most discussed events of the late 1890s in London, occupying columnists and journalists for years, was Isabella Stewart Gardner's purchase of Botticelli's *Chigi Madonna* (Cat. 1) and its export from Italy to America, with a brief stopover for exhibition in the British Isles.

With the dramatic rise in his popularity at the end of the nineteenth century came an attendant increase, no less dramatic, in the number of paintings bearing credible or unreasonably hopeful attributions to Botticelli that flooded the art market and appeared on the walls of prominent public collections. An unprecedented number of superficially critical studies of Botticelli's art were published to satisfy the appetites of an educated and curious reading public. At the same time, however, new archival research helped refine the outlines of Vasari's biography of Botticelli and corrected many of the dates and presumed facts about the artist's life that had long been taken for granted. Iconographers struggled to decode the mysterious layers of meaning that lay behind such paintings as the *Primavera*, *Pallas and the Centaur*, and the *Birth of Venus*. Serious connoisseurs labored to prune the inventories of incorrectly attributed works, to clarify the stages of the artist's development, and to define the nature of his relationships with his contemporaries. One of the most imaginative essays ever written by an art historian, Bernard Berenson's "Amico di Sandro," even invented a new and, it would ultimately prove, fictitious artist to explain why not just the worst but also some of the best paintings attributed to Botticelli revealed a wholly separate personality. All of these independent yet loosely related undertakings bore fruit, in 1908, in a book that has been called, aptly, "the best monograph in English on an Italian painter," Herbert P. Horne's *Botticelli, Painter of Florence*, a book that is as much a landmark in its field as its subject was within the history of Italian painting.

The strength of Horne's monograph lay in the breadth of its scholarship, the rigor of its method, the quality of its observations, and the balance and clear-sighted judgment of its conclusions; in all these respects it has rarely been equalled by any art historical publication. Yet it, too, was very much a product of its time, and as "the well from which later books on Botticelli one and all are drawn," it is important to understand the biases it presupposes and the misconceptions its author was seeking to redress. It was, for example, common in the nineteenth century to embroider on Vasari's claim that before being apprenticed to Fra Filippo Lippi, Botticelli had studied with a goldsmith named Botticello (from whom, Vasari said, he took his nickname); from this information scholars had indiscriminately ascribed the peculiar character of Botticelli's early Madonnas to the influence of either Andrea del Verrocchio or Antonio Pollaiuolo, the two leading goldsmith/painters of the preceding generation in Florence. Having discredited the myth of a goldsmith named Botticello, Horne went to great but unnecessary lengths to further prove that no trace of Verrocchio's influence could be discerned in any autograph painting by Botticelli. Only Pollaiuolo, he asserted categorically, with whom Botticelli is anyway known to have collaborated in 1470, could have made any decisive impression on the young artist. The trend of most modern scholarship, however, is to dismiss the Pollaiuolesque aspects of Botticelli's style as fortuitous—they are, in fact, common to many painters active in Florence at that time—and to search instead for a moment when Botticelli could have been an active member of Verrocchio's workshop. Several writers have even attributed to Botticelli, working alongside the young Leonardo da Vinci, a share in painting Verrocchio's altarpiece of the *Baptism of Christ*, now in the Uffizi, making it potentially the most auspicious collaborative undertaking in the history of Western culture.

Horne's primary ambition was to establish for Botticelli a restricted corpus of fully autograph works, stripping away the forest of misattributions and workshop productions of secondary quality to reveal the artist's personality in its purified essence. His gauge for doing so was the characteristic he found to be most salient and at the same time most difficult to imitate in Botticelli's universally acknowledged masterpieces: the draughtsmanship. "There is no drawing like Botticelli's," Ruskin had said, and Horne set out to make that critical observation into a scientific principle, using the strength and quality of line visible in any given painting as a litmus test for its authenticity. But the paradigm

Horne was working from was an anachronistic one, based on the nineteenth-century academic prototype of the master painter surrounded by a nebulous crowd of admiring students and imitators. It is now generally believed that the practical realities of a fifteenth-century painter's workshop were far more prosaic and commercial than this romantic model might suggest, and that Botticelli in particular perfected a near assembly-line approach to "manufacturing" works of art, thus making judgments of authenticity and appraisals of quality a tenuous and complicated task. Nonetheless, the thrust of nearly every monograph on Botticelli to have appeared since 1908 is an attempted revision of Horne's catalogue of autograph and studio productions, invariably proceeding from the same tenets he established in *Botticelli, Painter of Florence*. The most recent and the most comprehensive such monograph, Ronald Lightbown's *Sandro Botticelli* (1978), compiles synopses of critical opinion, pro and con, for every painting the author considers to be by or related to Botticelli. The result is as confusing and ultimately meaningless as such an exercise can be for any painter of the Italian Renaissance.

The greatest difficulties Horne encountered in applying his quality standards were presented by Botticelli's late works. Vasari had said of the artist, "Finally, having become old, unfit for work, and helpless, he was obliged to go on crutches, being unable to stand upright, and so he died, after long illness and decrepitude . . ." This part of Vasari's biography remains unsubstantiated, but Horne and all earlier writers on Botticelli understood the remark to be factual. The result was that Horne included only five small paintings, three of them from a single commission, among his catalogue of autograph works painted in the last decade of the artist's life, whereas he had accepted many times that number, including full-scale altarpieces and frescoes, for every decade earlier. Botticelli's late style remains a mystery for art historians. His harsh, almost brutal and deliberately unattractive manner of drawing, acidic palette, and confused compositions so contradict the elegance and lyrical naturalism of Botticelli's early works that most of the late paintings were—and often still are—thought to be eccentric pastiches of Botticelli's style executed by stiff and ungainly imitators. The tenaciousness of this idea is not surprising when it is recalled that the Botticelli championed by aesthetes of the late-nineteenth and early-twentieth centuries—the period of Art Nouveau—is the Botticelli who harmonized with the finest productions of modern design of that time, not the dark and troubled artist whom Vasari described as embracing the feverish ideas of Savonarola and his followers. Subsequent writers more sensitive to expressionism and better attuned to the emotional power of Botticelli's paintings have added a limited number of works to Horne's list, but, not rejecting his criteria of judgment, they could not radically revise his image of the artist's destitute and unproductive late years. Wholly convincing recent attributions, however, present a different picture of Botticelli's decline, suggesting that he continued to operate a productive studio that catered to a changing market. Demand for Botticelli's work certainly diminished, but it never disappeared entirely.

The two most frequently debated topics concerning the art and life of Sandro Botticelli involve his relationships with the two dominant political figures of his time: Lorenzo de' Medici, called il Magnifico, and Fra Girolamo Savonarola. Prior to his death in 1492, Lorenzo il Magnifico is thought to have been Botticelli's staunchest patron, commissioning from him the famous *Primavera* (Fig. 2), the *Birth of Venus* (Fig. 1), and the *Pallas and the Centaur* among other works, including the fresco decoration, now lost, of Lorenzo's villa Spedaletto near Volterra. Working on such privileged commissions, Botticelli is commonly supposed to have been in regular contact with the circle of distinguished poets, philosophers, and statesmen that surrounded Lorenzo, with the result that many of the paintings from the first half of Botticelli's career, especially those made for Lorenzo (who was himself a poet of not insignificant accomplishment), have been subjected to endlessly debated iconographic analyses intended to reveal layers of meaning more subtle than those expected of any other painter working anywhere in the fifteenth century.

After the death of Lorenzo il Magnifico, Botticelli is believed to have fallen under the baleful influence of the fanatical Dominican preacher Savonarola. Evidence to this effect is inconclusive. Vasari claims that Botticelli engraved illustrations to Savonarola's *Triumph of Faith*, though no copies of any such engravings are known to survive. Vasari further states that Botticelli became "so zealous a partisan [of Savonarola] that he totally abandoned painting, and not having any other means of living, he fell into very great difficulties." Botticelli's third brother, Simone, with whom the artist lived from 1493, was certainly a Savonarola sympathizer, and composed a chronicle of events recounting the Frate's ascendancy to power in Florence and his fall in 1498. Furthermore, much attention has been paid to Botticelli's work for known Savonarola followers, but it is unclear to what degree political convenience rather than religious conviction might be credited for this "allegiance." No sudden drop in artistic output occasioned by a conversion, as implied by Vasari, is evident from Botticelli's surviving works, and the change in the style of his art during the last half of his career is so gradual and continuous that it seems unlikely that a single outside source can be held responsible. Arguments that Botticelli concentrated exclusively on religious paintings at the end of his career are neither accurate nor relevant (see Cat. 10), as an artist's subjects in fifteenth-century Florence were dictated by his clients, not by his own personal interests.

It could be said that compared to the work of other fifteenth-century artists, the paintings of Sandro Botticelli have been studied to excess, but with results that are still frustratingly vague, confusing, and contradictory. It could also be said that compared to his paintings, his work in other media—including designs for embroideries, woodcuts, engravings, and intarsie—have barely been accorded the attention they deserve. Botticelli, in other words, is an artist who is far better known than understood. The workings of his mind, the channels of his patronage, the methods of his production are all subjects of inquiry only imperfectly explored. He has invited or endured such meandering levels of interpretation (most of it less illuminating of its subject than of the time at which it was written), and he has been the object of such uncritical popular adulation that it is difficult to approach his work with fresh eyes and an open mind. The purpose of this exhibition and catalogue is neither to write the definitive outline of Botticelli's artistic biography nor to present yet another testimonial to his place in the Western canon. It is to look again, if possible more closely, at "the peculiar sensation . . . the peculiar quality of pleasure which his work has the property of exciting in us, and which we cannot get elsewhere," more particularly to look at the sensations aroused by works available to generations of museum-goers in and around Boston, and to see whether these sensations bring any new questions or answers to mind.

Biographical Note

Sandro Botticelli was born Alessandro di Mariano Filipepi in Florence in 1445, one of a family of eight children. His father, Mariano di Giovanni d'Amadeo Filipepi, was a tanner of extremely modest circumstances, though his eldest brother, Giovanni, appears to have been a successful broker and to have borne the principal share of supporting the family. This brother was nicknamed "Il Botticello" (probably "the fat one"), and the epithet came to be used as a surname not only by his own children but also by his younger brothers. Sandro's second brother, Antonio, was trained as a goldsmith, specifically working as a goldbeater providing gold leaf to painters' studios; it was undoubtedly through him that Sandro was first introduced to the craft of painting. In 1458 his father returned a tax declaration stating that Sandro, a boy of thirteen, was at home learning to read. Probably soon afterwards he was apprenticed to Fra Filippo Lippi, at that time the most famous painter in Florence (Lippi actually lived in nearby Prato) and a favorite artist of the Medici.

The importance of Botticelli's apprenticeship with Filippo Lippi is fully apparent from studying his early paintings (see Cat. 1), but its duration is nowhere recorded. Nor has any association, either as a student or as a contractual assistant, with Andrea del Verrocchio been documented, but the influence of that versatile painter, sculptor, and goldsmith, who was also high in the favor of the Medici, is equally apparent in Botticelli's early paintings. Botticelli was probably practicing as a fully independent master in the late 1460s and certainly by 1470, when he is mentioned in a Florentine chronicle as the head of a workshop. In that year he was also paid for painting a figure of Fortitude for the magistrates of the Mercanzia, a commission he won in competition with Piero Pollaiuolo. Two years later, Botticelli enrolled in the Compagnia di San Luca, a religious confraternity comprised exclusively of painters and their studio associates, with Filippino Lippi, the son of Fra Filippo Lippi, listed as his apprentice.

Major paintings by Botticelli for Florentine churches and palaces are recorded at intervals throughout the last quarter of the fifteenth century, beginning in 1473/4 with a large *Saint Sebastian* for Santa Maria Maggiore, now in Berlin. In 1475 Botticelli was favored by Giuliano de' Medici with the commission to paint his standard for a much-heralded joust held in Piazza Santa Croce, and when, three years later, Giuliano was assassinated in the "Congiura dei Pazzi," Botticelli was selected to paint the effigies of the executed conspirators on the facade of the Palazzo Vecchio. Two fresco commissions followed shortly thereafter, one in 1480 for the church of the Ognissanti, where he painted a large figure of *Saint Augustine in his Study* in competition with Domenico Ghirlandaio, who painted a pendant Saint Jerome; and one in 1481 for the hospital of San Martino alla Scala, where he painted an Annunciation in an elaborate architectural setting. These led to Botticelli's appointment late in 1481 to fresco the walls of the newly completed Sistine Chapel at the Vatican. Working in company with three other artists—Pietro Perugino, Domenico Ghirlandaio, and Cosimo Rosselli—Botticelli contributed three large narrative frescoes to this extensive project, as well as several of the full-length papal portraits painted alongside the windows immediately beneath the ceiling.

Returned to Florence in 1482 from Rome, where he is said also to have painted an *Adoration of the Magi*, possibly to be identified with a painting now in the National Gallery of Art in Washington, Botticelli accepted a commission to fresco a wall in the Sala dei Gigli in the Palazzo della Signoria, a project that ultimately was not realized. The following year he collaborated with the painter Bartolomeo di Giovanni on four panels representing Boccaccio's story of Nastagio degli Onesti, commissioned to celebrate the marriage of Giannozzo di Antonio Pucci and Lucrezia Bini. In 1485 Botticelli painted an altarpiece for the Bardi Chapel in Santo Spirito, now in Berlin, and probably in 1489 an altarpiece of the

Annunciation for the Guardi chapel in Santa Maria Maddalena di Cestello, now in the Uffizi. This decade, probably the most productive of Botticelli's career, also saw the execution of several well-known but undocumented works that are difficult to date with precision, including the *Birth of Venus*, *Pallas and the Centaur*, and two tondi, the *Madonna of the Magnificat* and the *Madonna of the Pomegranate*, all in the Uffizi, the Villa Lemmi frescoes in the Louvre, and the *Mars and Venus* in the National Gallery, London.

The last two decades of Botticelli's life, though highly eventful, are documented by only a single signed and dated painting: the so-called *Mystical Nativity* in the National Gallery, London, finished early in 1501. The esteem in which he was held at this period may be suggested by notices of 1491, in which he was summoned to form part of a committee judging designs for the facade of the Cathedral in Florence; 1502, in which he was recommended to Isabella Gonzaga, duchess of Ferrara, as one of the principal painters of Florence; and 1504, when he was consulted over the placement of Michelangelo's statue of David. He is also documented working in the Chapel of Saint Zenobius in the Cathedral in 1491; in 1496 at the monastery of Santa Maria di Monticelli; and for Lorenzo di Pierfrancesco de' Medici at the Villas of il Trebbio and Castello in 1495 and 1497 (none of these works survives or can be securely identified). Numerous Madonna and Child compositions must also date from this period, as do such small but important paintings as the *Calumny of Apelles* and the *Saint Augustine* in the Uffizi, the *Last Communion of Saint Jerome* at the Metropolitan Museum of Art, New York, the four *Saint Zenobius* panels in New York, London, and Dresden, and the two moving images of the *Lamentation over the Dead Christ* in Milan and Munich.

Botticelli died on May 17, 1510, and was buried in the cemetery adjacent to the church of the Ognissanti in Florence.

Catalogue

A Note on the Catalogue

As was common in the practice of all but a few Florentine studios in the fifteenth century, Botticelli's paintings were mostly executed on wood panels to which the frame had been attached in advance. When these frames were removed by subsequent owners (none of the frames in the current exhibition is original to the object it contains), a border of unpainted wood was frequently left on all sides of the painted image. Dimensions recorded for panel paintings in this catalogue refer to the painted surface only; if the panel support is larger it will not be so indicated here; if the painted surface is irregular, the maximum height or width is recorded. In all cases, height precedes width in the measurements.

Catalogue 1

Sandro Botticelli (1445–1510)

Madonna and Child with an Angel, ca. 1472–1475
(also known as the *Chigi Madonna* or the *Madonna of the Eucharist*)
Tempera on panel
85.2 x 65 cm (33 1/2 x 25 5/8 in)
Isabella Stewart Gardner Museum, Boston
P27w73

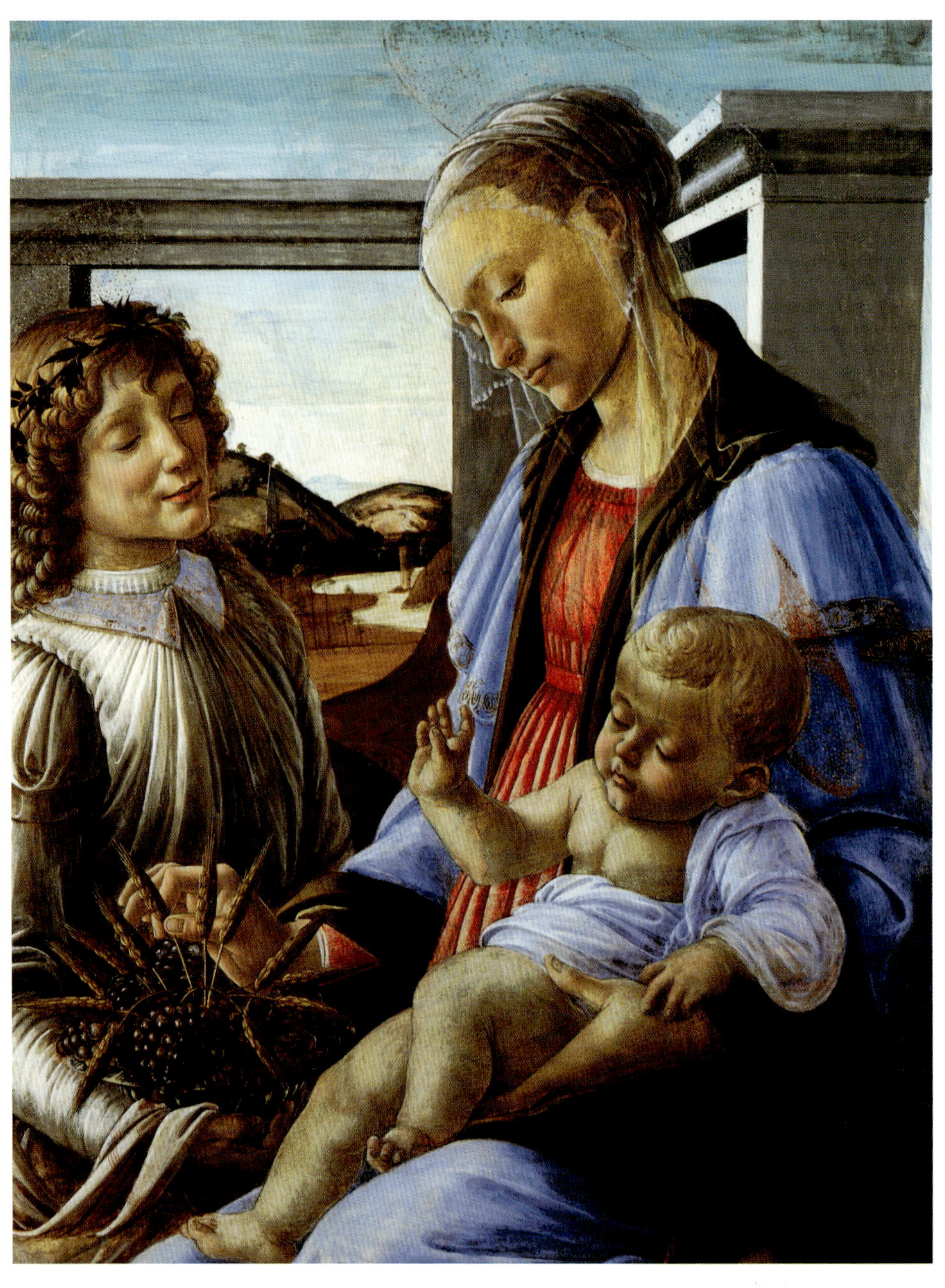

The overwhelming majority of paintings attributed to Botticelli's earliest period are all variations on a single subject: the Madonna and Child, presented either alone or with attendant angels, seated in an architectural interior or against an open landscape—or, as here, in an unresolved combination of the two. An almost limitless demand for this type of painting in Florence assured a young artist that he could produce them as objects for sale without having a specific patron or client in mind, enabling him to establish his reputation and garner more lucrative commissions for altarpieces or frescoes. Rarely were such paintings intended to convey a complicated meaning; they were meant only to introduce an image of the Christ Child and His mother into the home of its owner. The *Chigi Madonna*, however, is different in this respect. The bowl filled with grapes and ears of wheat that is held by the angel at the left has unmistakable eucharistic connotations, symbolizing the Christ Child's impending sacrifice as reenacted daily in the sacrifice of the Mass: the grapes (wine) are the blood of Christ and the wheat (bread) is His body, sanctified by the priest and offered in Communion to the congregation. In this picture, the Christ Child seems to take the place of the priest, sanctifying the bread and wine with His gesture of benediction, while the Virgin seems to accept Communion on behalf of all mankind. So intricate an allegory may imply that the *Chigi Madonna* was not conceived as a randomly composed image. Underdrawing now visible through thinning layers of paint even suggests that the angel and the Christ Child were moved farther apart than originally planned, perhaps to lay greater emphasis on the direction of their glances and gestures toward the eucharistic symbols. But if Botticelli was following the requirements of a specific commission, the name of his client, the painting's first owner, remains unknown.

Since its rediscovery in 1890, hanging on the ground floor of the Palazzo Chigi in Rome, the *Chigi Madonna* has been almost universally acclaimed as one of the great masterpieces of Botticelli's early career. Its sale by Prince Chigi and its export from Italy just before the turn of the century provoked a minor scandal in the European press, and its purchase by Isabella Stewart Gardner from Colnaghi, the reputable firm of London art dealers, was not made public until 1902. To this day it is admired as one of the singular landmarks of Italian Renaissance painting in any American collection. The painting is notable not only for the compelling humanity of its imagery, but also for its technical accomplishment, painted as it is in thin veils of nearly transparent color that give depth to the landscape and convey the warmth of the light striking the figures from the left. In it the artist achieves a carefully controlled balance of decorative and highly naturalistic details, as in the folds of the Virgin's dress, mantle, and veil or those of the angel's tunic and sleeves, which trace elegant arabesques while still capturing the essence of the fabric textures. All these characteristics are encountered only in the best of Botticelli's early works, yet they have come to be understood as the benchmarks of his style, making the *Chigi Madonna* one of the few paintings uncontroversially attributed to him.

The only lingering point of scholarly disagreement surrounding the *Chigi Madonna* concerns the date of its execution: was it one of Botticelli's very first efforts as an independent artist, painted in the middle or late 1460s, or is it a fully mature work, painted after the documented commissions of 1470 for the Arte della Mercanzia and 1474 for Santa Maria Maggiore? The dating of Botticelli's work has always been a contentious issue; his intellectual and technical development have resisted reduction to any formula that would satisfactorily account for the sequence of his paintings. The *Chigi Madonna* appears to be less closely based on the example of his first teacher, Fra Filippo Lippi, than are a number of other paintings attributed to Botticelli's earliest career, and it might therefore be presumed that it was not painted as early as the 1460s. The carefully modelled heads of all three figures in the painting, depicted by a light gliding smoothly over skin that reveals the full complexity of underlying bone and muscle structures, are probably more mature even than the *Fortitude* painted for the Mercanzia in 1470 (now in the Uffizi); they compare better to the *Saint Sebastian* of 1474 from Santa Maria Maggiore (now in Berlin). No other documented paintings by the artist are known from these years, however, so it is not possible to gauge how much earlier or later than 1474 the *Chigi Madonna* might have been designed or executed.

Catalogue 2

Nineteen engraved illustrations to the *Inferno* of Dante Alighieri, ca. 1481–1485, after designs by Botticelli

For a full listing of the nineteen engraved illustrations see the Appendix to Catalogue 2, page 61.

2a. *La Commedia di Dante*
with a commentary by Cristoforo Landino, published in Florence, 1481, by Niccolo di Lorenzo della Magna
Bound book
41.1 x 26.6 cm (16 1/4 x 10 1/2 in)
Opened to *The Banks of the Phlegethon: The Punishments of Sodomy: The Cord Dropped into the Pit: Geryon*
(illustration to the *Inferno*, Canto XVI)
Isabella Stewart Gardner Museum, Boston
2.c.1/8

2b. *Dante Lost in the Wood, Escaping, and Meeting Virgil*
(illustration to the *Inferno*, Canto I)
Engraving
9.5 x 17.3 cm (3 3/4 x 6 5/8 in)
Fogg Art Museum
Harvard University Art Museums
Gray Collection of Engravings Fund, G7835

2c. *Dante and Virgil, with the Vision of Beatrice*
(illustration to the *Inferno*, Canto II)
Engraving
9.6 x 17.4 cm (3 3/4 x 6 5/8 in)
Fogg Art Museum
Harvard University Art Museums
Gift of Paul J. Sachs, M667

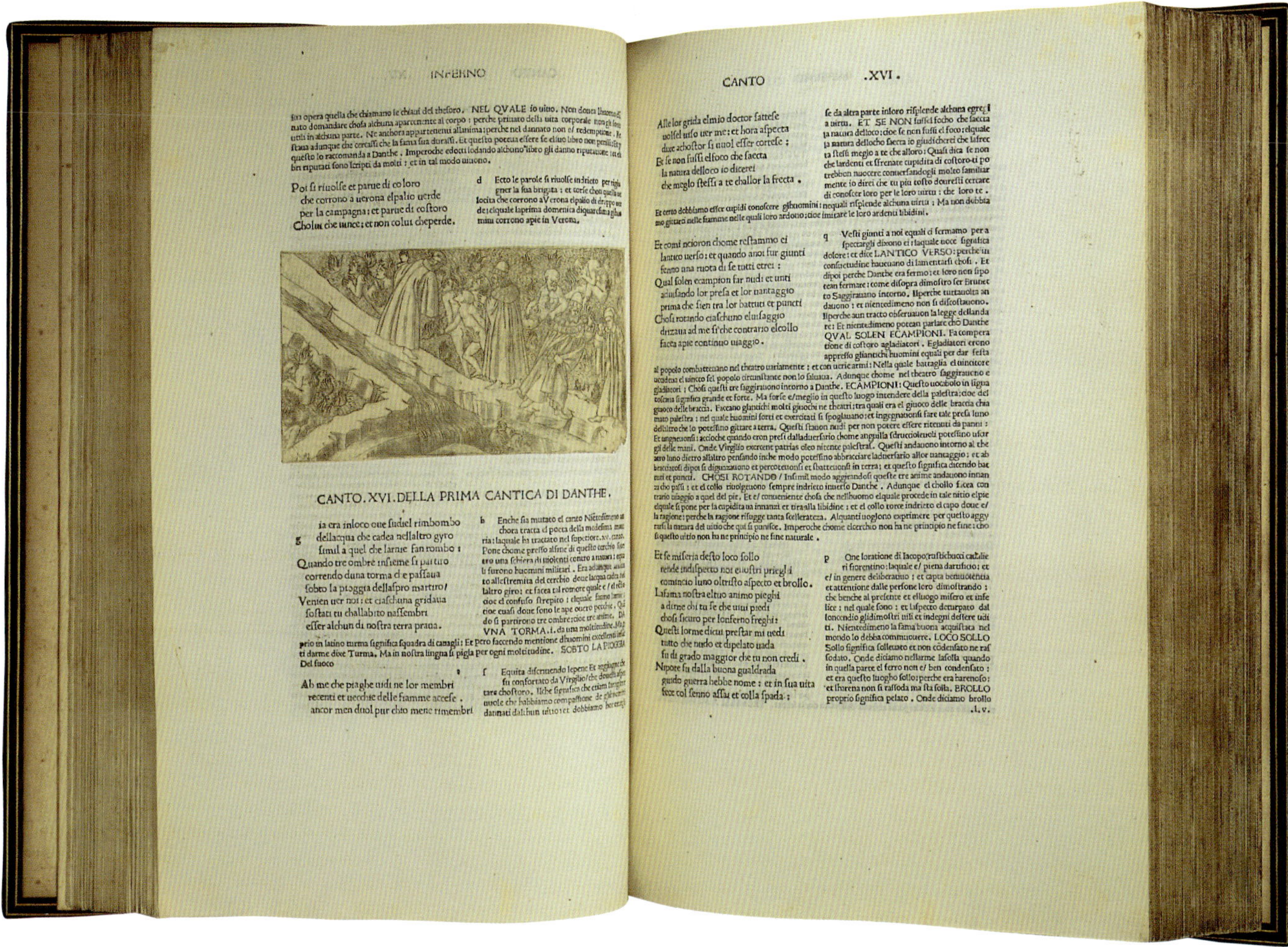
INFERNO

CANTO .XVI.

CANTO.XVI.DELLA PRIMA CANTICA DI DANTHE.

Catalogue 2A.

La Commedia di Dante

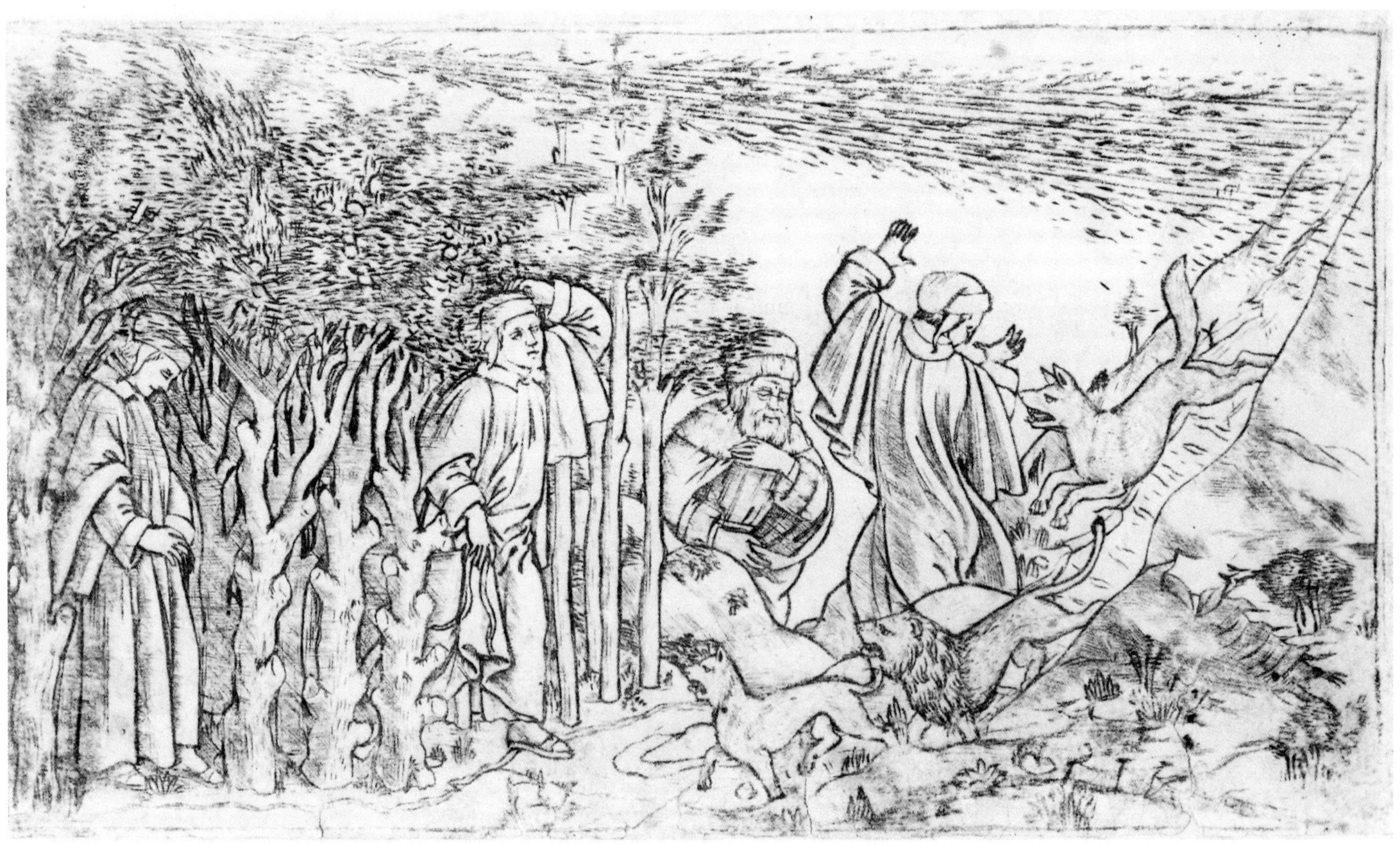

Catalogue 2B. *Dante Lost in the Wood, Escaping, and Meeting Virgil*

On August 30, 1481, a German printer in Florence, Niccolo di Lorenzo della Magna (d'Alemagna), issued the first printed edition of Dante's *Divine Comedy* to be published in the poet's native city. This ambitious project, which included a newly expurgated text, the commentary of Cristoforo Landino, and a long preamble describing the state of the arts and letters in Florence, was also remarkable for being one of the first attempts to incorporate copperplate engravings, rather than woodcuts, as illustrations printed directly on the pages of the text (printing copperplate engravings and movable type require two different kinds of press). The experiment was only partially successful and illustrations were provided for only nineteen of the one hundred cantos of the poem.

Following a passage in Vasari's *Lives*, these nineteen engravings have always been understood to be based on drawings provided by Botticelli:

> Having completed the work assigned to him [in the Sistine Chapel, Botticelli] returned at once to Florence, where, being whimsical and eccentric [*this could perhaps be better translated as* ingenious *or* sophistical], he occupied himself with commenting on a certain part of Dante, illustrating the *Inferno*, and executing prints, over which he wasted much time, and, neglecting his proper occupation, he did no work, and thereby caused infinite disorder in his affairs.

Though it is recognized that Botticelli did not actually write a commentary on Dante, it is clear that he was responsible for designing the nineteen engravings illustrating the Landino text of 1481, as well as for executing a nearly complete set of illuminations on vellum illustrating the entire *Divine Comedy*, a work that was apparently produced late in his career for Lorenzo di Pierfrancesco de' Medici. The latter illuminations, which are now divided between museums in Berlin and the Vatican, are mostly uncolored and so could more accurately be described as detailed drawings. Each is a large and complex visualization of multiple episodes within the canto it illustrates, while the drawings prepared for the 1481 engravings must have been far simpler and more easily legible, reducing each canto to its key elements. The engravings themselves are relatively coarse and convey little of the subtlety of Botticelli's draughtsmanship, but they recognizably reflect his inventions and reveal one of the outstanding peculiarities of his style: the disparity between the care he lavished on the spatial illusion of his settings and the apparent disregard with which he positioned his figures within those settings to develop his narrative. In contrast to the naturalistic concerns evident in his monumental paintings, the small-scale narratives of Botticelli's book illustrations are nearly hieroglyphic in their urgent need to condense the story and convey its essential meaning, thus focusing attention on the emotional significance of the images.

INFERNO

eo muouerſi/ſe prima non ſi muoue la ragione. Entrai per lo camino alto: cioe profondo/chome diciamo alto mare et alto fiume; perche el primo camino fu per linferno cioe per la cognitione de uitii; equali ſono infimi: perche ſempre conſiſtono circa le choſe terrene. ET SILueſtro: perche chome dicemo nel principio epeccati naſcono dalla ſelua cioe dalla materia che e/elcorpo.

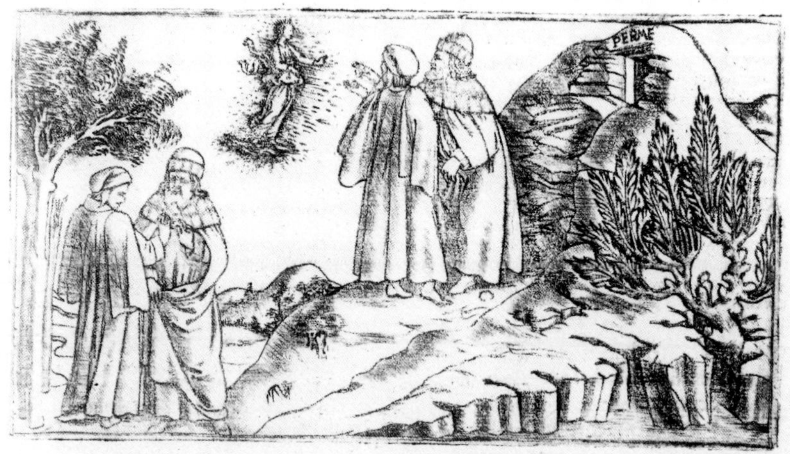

CANTO TERTIO DELLA PRIMA CANTICA

P Er me ſi ua nella citta dolente
per me ſi ua nelletherno dolore
per me ſi ua tra laperduta gente
Iuſtitia moſſe el mio alto factore
fecemi la diuina poteſtate
la ſomma ſapientia el primo amore
Dinanzi a me non fur choſe create
ſe non etherne et io etherno duro
laſciate ogni ſperanza uoi chentrate
Queſte parole di colore obſcuro
uidio ſcripte al ſommo duna porta
perchio maeſtro el ſenſo lor me duro.

S Ono alchuni equali credonoche edue primi capitoli ſieno ſtati inluoghi di proemio; et queſto terzo ſia el principio della narratione. Ma ſe conſiderremo chon diligentia tutta la materia/facilmente ſi puo prouare che la narratione comincia nel primo capitolo: et nel uerſo Io non ui ſo ben dire chomio uentrai. Imperoche Danthe narra in queſta ſua peregrinatione eſſer ſi ritrouato nella ſelua; et hauere ſmarrito la uia Eſſerſi condocto appie del monte. Et dipoi eſſerſi addirizato uerſo el ſole per erto camino elquale lo conduceua aſaluamento ſe le tre fiere non laueſſino ripincto al baſſo. Et finalmente ridocto quaſi al fondo hauere hauuto el ſoccorſo di Virgilio et dalle tre donne. Et p leſue parole eſſer pſuaſo laſciãdo el corto ãdare del mõte ſeguitarlo per linferno et purgatorio; laqual uia ſanza ſiniſtro intoppo lo puo conducere al cielo. Ilche ſignifica quello che gia diſopra habbiamo dimoſtro. Et ſe alchuno diceſſi che in amendue queſti canti molte choſe ſcriue conle quali capta ben uolẽtia et attẽtione et docilita: E non ſi uieta che ĩ ogni pte del poema non ſi poſſi fare queſto. Anzi maximamẽte ſirichiede allo ſcriptore che le capti douũque truoua occaſione di poterlo fare. Hora perche ſiamo gia al puncto chel poeta deſcende nellinferno. Giudico ſia utile exprimere che choſa ſia inferno; et in quanti modi ſi dica alchuno ſcendere allinferno. Inferno adunque e/linfima: et baſſa parte del mondo/decto inferno da queſta dictione infra che ſignifica diſocto: Ne ſolamente dal popolo di dio e/poſto lonferno: Ma anchora da molti poeti: et maxime da Homero da Virgilio. Ouidio. Statio; et Claudiano: Et molto piu egregiamente dal principe de philoſophi Platone/Coſtui incritone nel qual libro induce Socrate diſputante della immortalita dellanimo/dimoſtra che lanime humane dopo la morte ſono giudicate ſecondo le loro colpe: et nellonferno tormentate inſino atanto che ſi purghino/ſe epeccati non ſono ſtati molto graui. Ma quelle che hanno commeſſo ſcelerateze enorme: et ſono impurgabili ſecondo lui/ſono mandate in luogho piu profondo decto tartaro et quiui ſono afflicte inetherno con grauiſſimi ſupplicii. La quale oppinione e/molto ſimile alla chriſtiana fede; et abbraccia lonferno el purgatorio: Et la maggior pte

Catalogue 2C. *Dante and Virgil, with the Vision of Beatrice*

Canto I of the *Inferno*, beginning with the unforgettable lines "Nel mezzo del cammin di nostra vita/ mi ritrovai per una selva oscura," describes how Dante finds himself lost in a dark and savage wood. At the far left of his plate, Botticelli shows the poet brooding in thought or fear or even sleepiness—all three are suggested at different moments in the canto—within the deep shade of a bower of tightly interlaced branches. Coming to the foot of a hill, he looks up to see its summit bathed in the rays of the sun, a sight which gives him hope and eases his oppressive fear of the forest. For Dante, the sun's rays are a symbol of Divine radiance, and Botticelli gives them an almost corporeal presence, cutting across the top of the plate like bolts of flame as Dante, at the center, shields his eyes from their brilliance. Dante is prevented from climbing the hill first by a leopard, then by a lion, and finally by a ravenous wolf who chases him back into the gloom of the valley. There he encounters the ghost of the poet Virgil, whom he begs to show him the way to safety.

The four figures included by Botticelli in his illustration to Canto I each represents a different state of mind—two of them turbulent and two introspective—and they are disposed in a sequence, reading left to right, and in poses that reenact a highly descriptive and eventful narrative. Canto II of the poem offered Botticelli less opportunity either for portraying action or for expressing moods. In this canto, Dante doubts that he is worthy of the path to safety offered by Virgil, a journey through Hell and Purgatory to reach Paradise. Virgil reassures him by explaining that he was sent specifically to Dante's aid by Beatrice, who was herself commissioned on his behalf by the Virgin and Saint Lucy. In his illustration, Botticelli could do little more than show the great poets in conversation: once at the left, where Dante explains his doubts and fears, and once in the center, where Virgil recounts his vision of Beatrice come down from Heaven to summon him to the task. The setting of the print at the right is entirely deduced from the last line of the canto: "intrai per lo cammino alto e silvestro" [I entered on the steep and savage path]. It shows the rocky, broken ascent of a barren hill, topped with a gateway and the partial inscription, *"Per me"* [through me], a scene that is actually described only in Canto III.

In the engravings illustrating Cantos I and II, great care was taken to suggest the natural effects of light through shading of varying densities. The extremely fine parallel and crosshatched lines (from which the so-called "Fine Manner" technique, of which these prints are examples, derives its name) convincingly recreate the delicate wash of color shadings that must have enlivened Botticelli's original drawings. Furthermore, they show Botticelli, at this early stage of his career, still intent on creating unified, believable spaces, even to the extent of lighting the back of the hill at the right of his second plate to maintain the consistency of his light source, though this insistence compromises the narrative by casting the path and gate in deep shadow. In the remaining prints of the series, Botticelli was not quite as scrupulous about obeying the laws of natural phenomena when they conflicted with the demands of the story. Thus, for example, the gate to Hell in Canto III is brightly lit though it opens in the shadowed side of a rock wall. In Canto XVIII, Dante and Virgil are seen illuminated from behind with the fronts of their robes and caps properly cast in shadow; their faces, however, are fully lit. In general, light and shade in these later engravings are intended to indicate local modelling rather than atmospheric effects. Similarly, figure scale is rarely coordinated in any given scene to suggest recession into depth; rather, variations in size seem to be dependent either on a figure's relative importance to the story or on the amount of space in the design Botticelli needed to fill.

The publication date inscribed in the colophon of the Landino text, August 30, 1481, is generally taken to be the approximate date for Botticelli's designs as well. Several theories have been advanced to explain why the project was left uncompleted. The most common suggestion is that Botticelli broke off work on his designs when he was called to Rome in the summer of 1481 to paint in the Sistine Chapel, and that the publisher, despairing of his return, released the book with only the nineteen finished engravings. Such a theory does not address the evident difference in style between the first two engravings and the other seventeen, however, nor does it explain a number of technical peculiarities. Of the more than eighty copies of the Landino *Dante* known to survive, nearly half include only the first two engravings; not more than twenty include all nineteen. In those volumes that are complete, only the first two or three engravings are printed directly on the page with the text; the others are pasted into blank spaces at the beginning of each canto. Some books include two impressions of the engraving for Canto II—one printed in its correct place and another printed at the beginning of Canto III (in the Gardner copy, the correct illustration to Canto III is pasted *over* the second impression of Canto II). Five of the complete copies also include an alternate version of the illustration for Canto III that is clearly engraved in a different workshop; it is sometimes pasted into its proper place and sometimes tipped in at the beginning of Canto XX.

While it is difficult to imagine any reason for the existence of an alternate version of Plate 3, the most convincing explanation for the other irregularities proposes that the Landino *Dante* was first released in August 1481 with only two engraved illustrations. The other plates would then have been prepared after the first printing and pasted into unsold copies by the publisher. If this was indeed the case, Botticelli could have worked on the design of Plates 3 through 19 anytime after his return from Rome in 1482 (as Vasari in fact maintained), though nothing about their figure style suggests that they occupied him much past the middle of that decade. Another reason the series may have been abandoned incomplete could be the death, in 1487, of the craftsman assumed to have engraved the plates, the goldsmith Baccio Baldini. Almost nothing is known about Baldini except that Vasari says he was a follower of Maso Finiguerra, the supposed inventor of the technique of copperplate engraving (see Cat. 7), and that he worked primarily from drawings by Botticelli. His name has been associated on this meager evidence with as many as half of the surviving "Fine Manner" prints from the 1460s, 1470s, and 1480s, but first and foremost with the illustrations to the Landino *Dante*, the only prints executed in this technique that clearly betray the hand of Sandro Botticelli in their design.

Catalogue 3

Sandro Botticelli (1445–1510)

The Nativity, ca. 1482–1485
Tempera and oil on panel
79.6 cm (31 5/8 in) diameter
Isabella Stewart Gardner Museum, Boston
P27e1

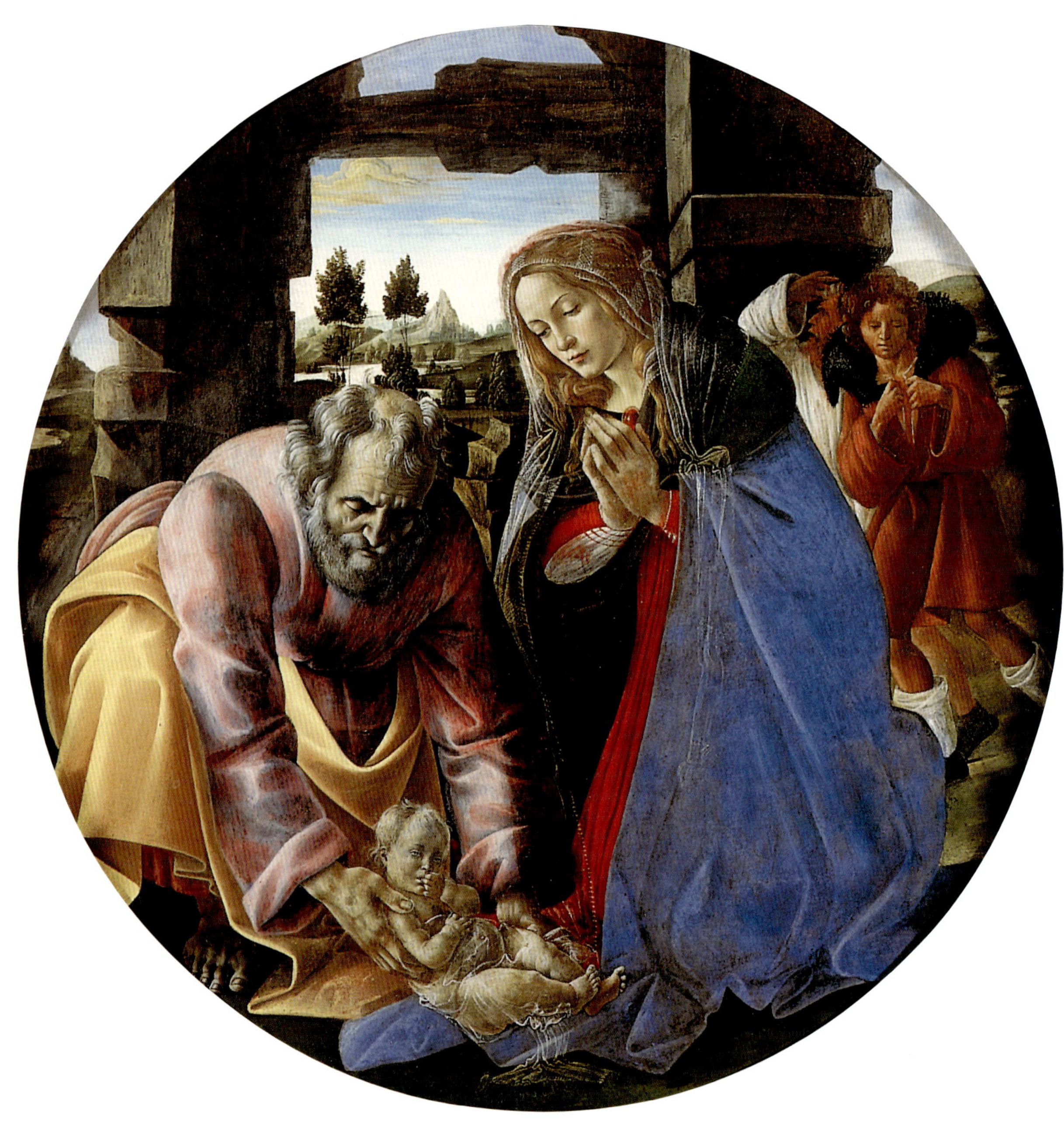

Tondi (round paintings) were among the most fashionable and expensive furnishings in fifteenth-century Florentine homes. Much costlier than rectangular paintings, presumably because their frames were much more difficult to construct and carve, they came to assume the role of a status symbol among upper-middle class families in Tuscany (their popularity in Italy was largely restricted to Florence and Siena and their dependencies), where wealthier households and even public institutions commissioned large, opulent examples from well-known artists, while less prosperous buyers contented themselves with replicated versions from less exalted workshops. Typically, a tondo was painted with an overtly domestic or familial subject appropriate for contemplation in the home, the most popular subjects being the Holy Family, the Nativity, and the Adoration of the Magi.

Botticelli outpaced most of his contemporaries in supplying the demand for these objects. Many of his most admired compositions were designed as tondi, apparently on commission from the upper end of the Florentine market; among them are several elaborate images of the Madonna and Child with angels, such as the so-called *Madonna of the Pomegranate* and the *Madonna of the Magnificat*, both in the Uffizi, and of the Adoration of the Magi, such as the large panel in the National Gallery, London. In these paintings, Botticelli generally arranged the figures to make the best or most decorative use of the circular picture area. He sometimes also exploited spatial devices creating the illusion of a convex surface—deeper towards the center and shallower at the edges—probably intended to evoke the effect of mirrors, which in fifteenth-century Florence were nearly all round and convex. Botticelli was equally adept at producing modest-sized tondi and at converting cartoons devised for a rectangular format to a circular one (see Cat. 9). He may also have sold his cartoons to other workshops for increased production. Many of his tondi, like most of his rectangular Madonna and Child compositions, survive in multiple replicas of varying degrees of quality, and Vasari recounts the story of one of Botticelli's pupils copying one of the master's tondi to sell for his own profit, with Botticelli's approval and even with his assistance in arranging the sale.

The Gardner tondo has been the subject of the widest possible range of critical opinion. Most scholars consider it a late work, painted close to 1495 and with extensive intervention from Botticelli's studio. Some authors have noted a difference within the painting between the fine-featured elegance of the Virgin and the massive, heavy-limbed solidity of Saint Joseph, ascribing the former to Botticelli (or to an assistant working from Botticelli's drawings) and the latter to a second, unrelated artist, who has even been identified with such powerful figures of a younger generation as Luca Signorelli and Michelangelo Buonarotti. Some writers also argue that the landscape and the two shepherds in the right middle-ground were added to the composition at a later date, perhaps as late as the mid-sixteenth century.

Nothing about the Gardner tondo, however, suggests that assistants were involved in its execution in any but the most perfunctory manner—in brushing in parts of the background, for example. Furthermore, nothing about it supports the late date proposed by most scholars. Its figure types and drawing style correspond to paintings produced close in time to the frescoes in the Sistine Chapel (1481–1482), while the action and attitude of the two shepherds in the right middle-ground were clearly developed out of studies, probably of the same date, for the figures of Dante and Virgil illustrating the later Cantos of the *Inferno* (see Cat. 2). Saint Joseph's chiselled features and raw-boned hands—so unlike the ineffable grace and nobility of Botticelli's youthful male figures as to permit some writers to attribute him to another artist—first appear in the Ognissanti *Saint Jerome* of 1480 and reappear little changed in the Bardi altarpiece of 1485 and in the approximately contemporary San Barnaba altarpiece. The Gardner tondo was probably painted between these two dates, sometime in the first half of the 1480s.

Many of the difficulties scholars have experienced in reading this painting may be explained in part by its poor condition, for it has suffered over the centuries both from the overzealous attentions of restorers, who have abraded its surface and added disfiguring repaints, and from the instability of its own medium. For some reason, Botticelli used two different grounds to prepare different sections of the painting. The Virgin, for example, is painted over a typical terra-verde ground, commonly used by painters in the Renaissance to lend opacity and brightness to the color of flesh tones and draperies. Saint Joseph and the Christ Child, on the other hand, are painted over an unusual dark ground, and with the abrasion of surface layers of pigment that ground has become visible, lending a smoldering, mysterious depth to shadows and exaggerating the contrast of highlights in ways that were not intended. Furthermore, Saint Joseph's left sleeve is painted on top of the folds of the Virgin's mantle and dress, suggesting that he was added to the composition (which without him resembles that of another tondo by Botticelli now in Piacenza) relatively late in its development. Perhaps he was painted over an area originally intended for the Christ Child alone, for the Virgin's gaze is not directed at the spot on which her Son actually lies. The two shepherds at the right were probably also added later; they are now cropped uncomfortably by the Virgin's left shoulder and one of them gazes upward, presumably at a Star of Bethlehem—though none is included anywhere within the picture field. The sequence of these alterations and the reasons for them are unclear; perhaps they were intended simply to change a traditional scene of the Adoration of the Christ Child into a Nativity. It may be noted that while Botticelli experimented frequently with compositions showing the Virgin adoring the Christ Child, only three other tondi of the Nativity by him are known—one in the Faringdon Collection, Buscot Park; one in the Blaffer Collection, Houston; and one in the North Carolina Museum of Art, Raleigh—and all of these were painted at the end of his career, fifteen to twenty years after the Gardner tondo.

Sandro Botticelli (1445–1510) and Studio

Christ the Redeemer (Salvator Mundi), ca. 1490
Tempera on linen
57.1 x 34.9 cm (22 1/2 x 13 3/4 in)
Fogg Art Museum
Harvard University Art Museums
Gift of the Friends of the Fogg Museum of Art Fund, 1930.2

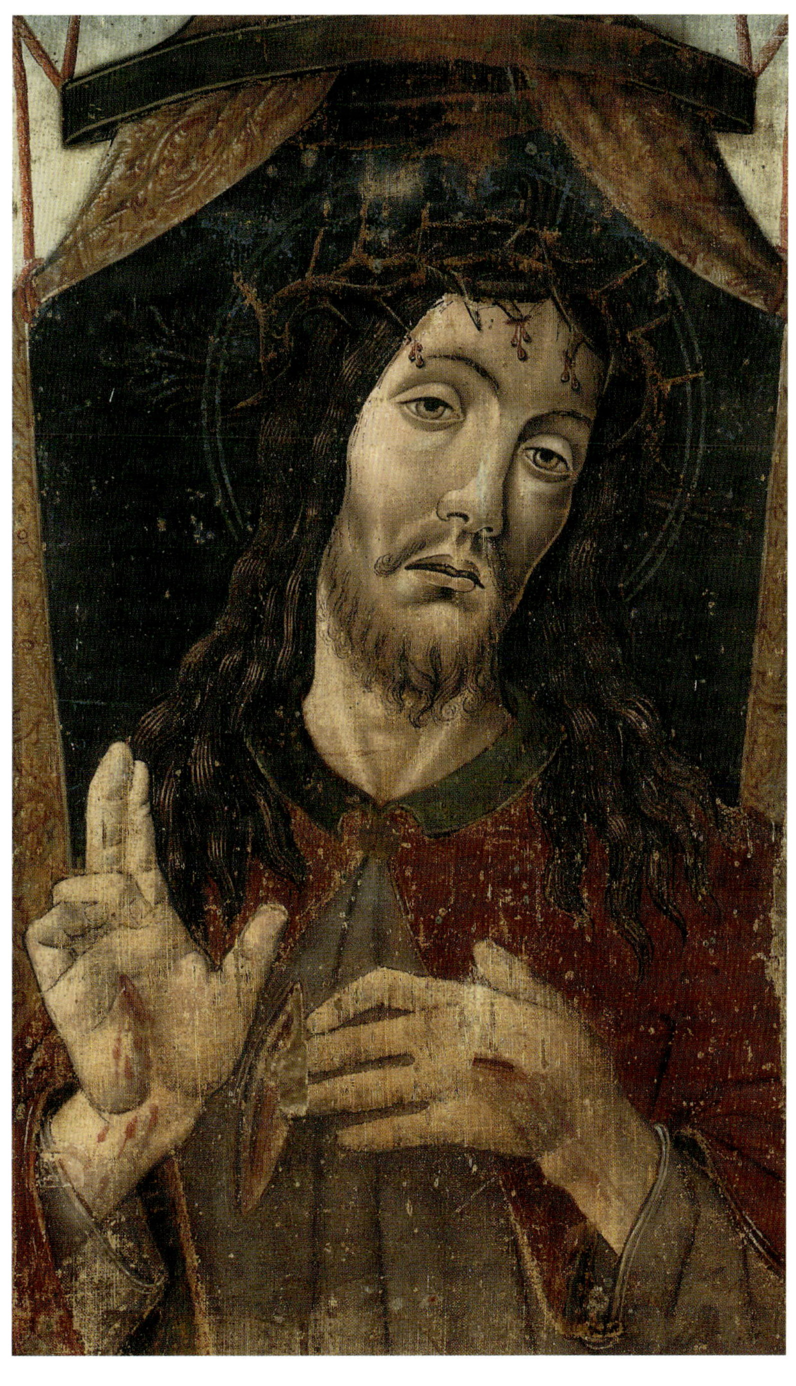

Belying the simplicity of its appearance, Botticelli's *Christ the Redeemer* is a complicated image that conflates two separate visual traditions. Bust-length paintings of Christ as the Savior of the World (Salvator Mundi) show Him with His right hand raised in blessing and His left holding a globe, a symbol of power and majesty; such images, which were common in Europe throughout the fifteenth century, were meant to inspire awe and reverence in the onlooker. Even more common in Northern Europe, if relatively scarce in Italy, were images of Christ as the Man of Sorrows. Meant to inspire not awe but pity, such images typically portray Christ crowned with thorns, sometimes mourned by angels or the Virgin and Saint John the Evangelist, and sometimes surrounded by the instruments of the Passion, symbols of His torment and sacrifice. Only a few examples are known where these two disparate images are combined to show Christ as the Man of Sorrows raising His hand in benediction. One painted by Giovanni Bellini, now in the Louvre, is a highly detailed and labored image, presenting a stooped and weary, very naturalistic Christ standing before a very believable landscape. Botticelli's instead reduces the subject to its barest essentials, creating an image of almost hieroglyphic simplicity that would communicate its pietistic, devotional message as effectively and as urgently if translated into a line engraving or woodcut as it does as a painting.

Like a woodcut or engraving, Botticelli's image was intended for replication, both by assistants in his own studio, who worked from a cartoon prepared by the master, and by artists in other studios, such as Jacopo del Sellaio, who copied Botticelli's paintings or drawings, presumably with his approval. One of the finest of the many surviving replicas and variants of this image is the painting on linen now in the Fogg Art Museum at Harvard University. It corresponds almost line for line to another version of significant quality, painted on panel, now in the Accademia Carrara at Bergamo (Fig. 6), and, less closely, to a variant now in the Detroit Institute of Arts. All these images, and numerous others that add ancillary details such as one or more of the instruments of the Passion, were intended to stimulate private devotion and meditation on Christ's suffering. The Detroit and Bergamo panels both have black backgrounds, eliminating the distractions from their principal subject that might have been caused by a landscape or architectural setting. The version in the Fogg adds a baldachin and parted drapes hung on ropes behind the bust of Christ, lending it the appearance of a reliquary or monstrance being exposed for the veneration of a congregation.

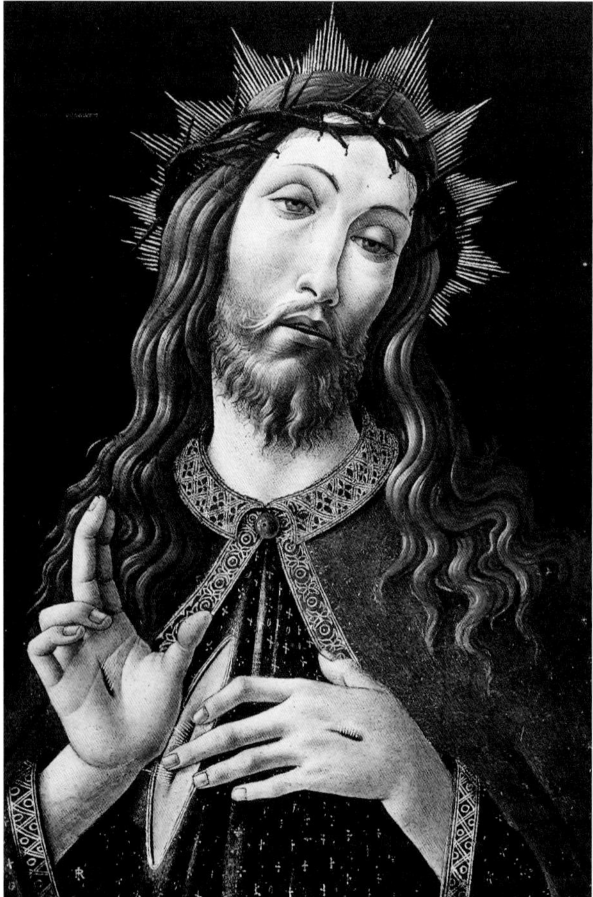

Figure 6. *Man of Sorrows*. Bergamo, Accademia Carrara.

The Fogg Redeemer is unusual for being painted on unprimed linen. This medium was usually reserved for processional standards and other objects that needed to be lightweight for portability, but since it is such a fragile medium it is possible that it was once far more commonly employed than the rare surviving examples might otherwise imply. Damage visible throughout the paint surface of the Fogg Redeemer, entirely consistent with the fragility of unprimed linen, complicate questions of attribution and dating that are in any event problematic for an object intended from the first to be a replica. The bust of Christ was presumably traced onto the linen by Botticelli or one of his assistants, probably using the same cartoon employed for the Bergamo panel. It may then have been partially or fully colored in by an assistant (the baldachin and halo were unquestionably added by an assistant), with Botticelli adding touches of modelling to the surface, which would now be largely effaced. It is unlikely that the painting ever boasted much more illusionistic detail, such as delicate cast shadows, than it now displays, so the need for Botticelli's personal intervention would have been limited. Though a date as early as 1482 has been suggested for the version of this composition now in Detroit, the Bergamo and Fogg paintings are unlikely to have been designed earlier than the San Barnaba altarpiece of the middle or late 1480s, as they borrow something of their postures and expressive mood from the figure of Saint John the Baptist in that painting. Whether they were executed immediately after the altarpiece or sometime in the 1490s, as most scholars seem to think, is purely a matter of conjecture.

Catalogue 5

Francesco Botticini (1446–1497)

Virgin and Child with the Young Saint John the Baptist, ca. 1470–1480

Tempera on panel

67 x 47.3 cm (26 3/8 x 18 5/8 in)

Isabella Stewart Gardner Museum, Boston

P16w21

In addition to the stories, anecdotes, and witticisms he recorded, Giorgio Vasari included in his biography of Botticelli a list of the artist's major public works. Two of these, a tabernacle at Empoli and an altarpiece of the Assumption of the Virgin commissioned by the writer Matteo Palmieri (1406–1475), are now known to have been painted not by Botticelli but by Francesco Botticini. Vasari apparently confused the spelling of the two artists' names, which may have been recorded in locally available documents or in an inscription on the altarpiece frame, thus guaranteeing the obscurity of Francesco Botticini as an historical figure until the last decade of the nineteenth century, when German scholars began to identify works that could be attributed to him. Though an artist of modest ambitions, Botticini would have enjoyed some posthumous notoriety had it not been for Vasari's mistake. The Palmieri altarpiece, then in San Pier Maggiore and now exhibited at the National Gallery, London, enjoyed a *succès de scandale* when Matteo Palmieri, shortly after his death, was accused of heresy. The altarpiece, which illustrates some doctrinally questionable passages in one of Palmieri's poems, was covered with a veil, and Vasari went to some lengths to rail at narrow-minded critics who accused Botticelli (sic) of complicity in heresy for having painted it.

Francesco Botticini served a brief apprenticeship (1459) in the studio of one of the most prolific and conservative painters in Florence, Neri di Bicci. He seems to have patterned his own career on Neri's, catering to a modest segment of the art market that was content with unadventurous, repetitive works of art—primarily paintings of the Madonna and Child or the Nativity—that were executed with solid craftsmanship and pleasing, decorative compositions. His style betrays an amalgamation of influences, compounded at will, from a number of artists including Andrea del Castagno, Fra Filippo Lippi, and especially Andrea del Verrocchio and Botticelli.

The Gardner Madonna, though severely abraded and therefore lacking much of the refinement of surface detail it must once have had, is typical of the best work associated with Botticini's name from the first half of his career. Its composition and figure types are loosely based on, and meant to recall, two of Botticelli's early Madonna and Child paintings from around 1470, one now in Naples and one in London, with the addition, behind them, of an airy, fanciful landscape that imitates the panoramic views made popular shortly before by Alesso Baldovinetti and Antonio Pollaiuolo. Eclectic combinations like this found an appreciative audience in Florence—an audience that was also exploited, though in different ways, by artists like Jacopo del Sellaio and even Botticelli himself. Botticelli frequently painted (or had painted by his assistants) copies of his own compositions with a variety of backgrounds available for different clients. A fine example is the beautiful Madonna and Child in the Fogg Art Museum, the two main figures of which are copied from the San Barnaba altarpiece of the mid-1480s, painted against a background developed from a pattern book of studies of Flemish Gothic architecture.

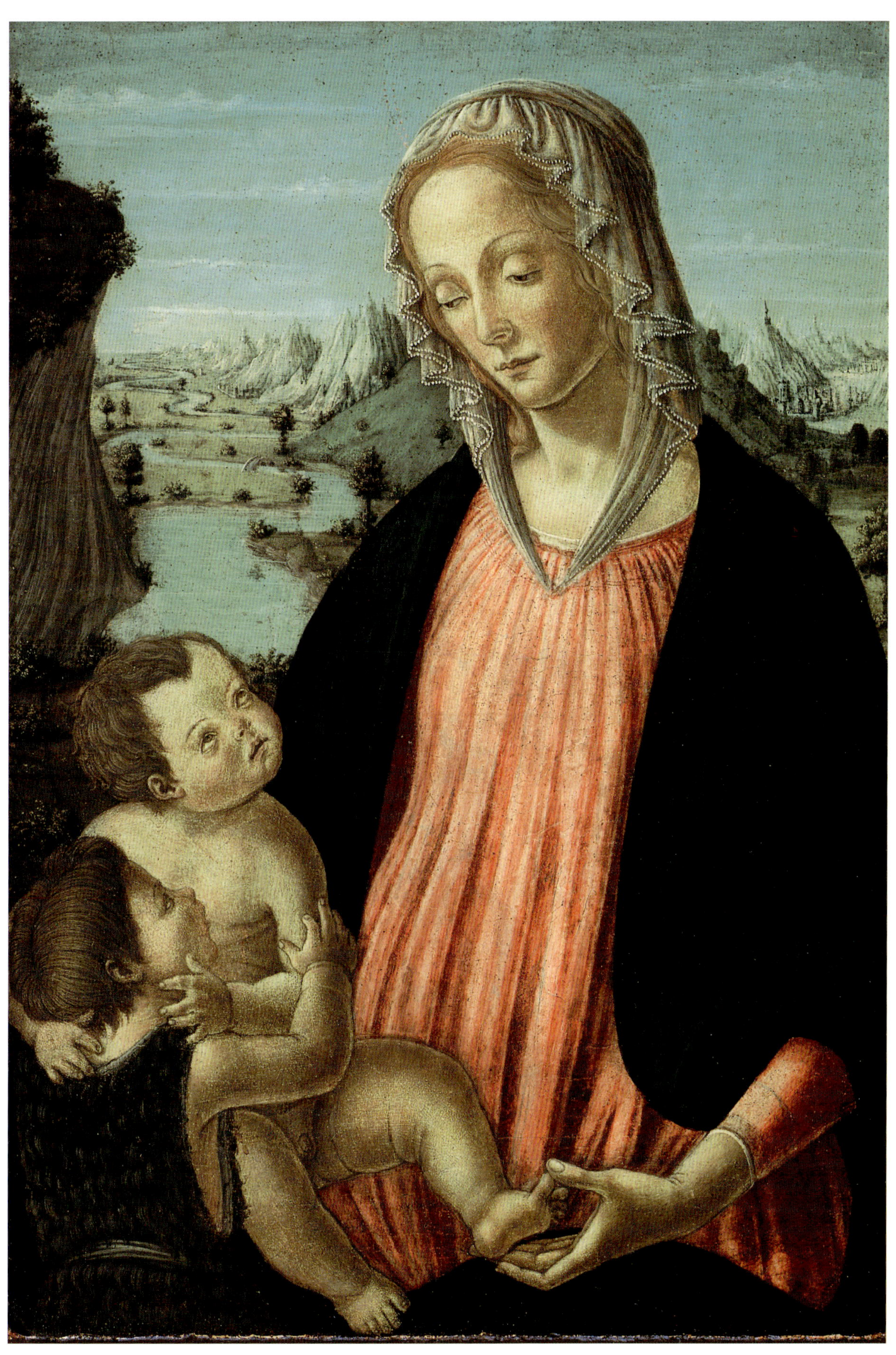

Catalogue 6

Jacopo del Sellaio (1441/2–1493)

The Story of Psyche, ca. 1490
Tempera and oil on panel
42 x 151.8 cm (16 9/16 x 59 3/4 in)
Museum of Fine Arts, Boston
Picture Fund, 12.1049

Prominent among the furnishings in wealthy Florentine homes of the fifteenth century were long, low chests called *cassoni*. Typically commissioned in pairs for a bride's trousseau, most *cassoni* were painted on their front face with narrative scenes from the Bible or from classical history or poetry, their subjects often chosen for their edifying moral content or as an augury for a good and virtuous marriage. Two examples of intact *cassoni* are on view in the Raphael Room in the Isabella Stewart Gardner Museum. Sellaio's *Story of Psyche* was cut from the front of one such chest. It shares with many *cassone* panels a complicated narrative structure, weaving several episodes from a single story into a unified landscape that fills a long, horizontal picture field. Like many *cassoni*, it is liberally decorated with gold, picking out highlights and details of the architecture and fabrics in an ostentatious display of the prosperity of its original owners. And like nearly all *cassoni*, it shows more damage within a semicircle around the top center of the panel than elsewhere—the result of keys on a ring banging against the front of the chest while it was being locked or unlocked. The Boston *Story of Psyche* was painted close to 1490, relatively late in the tradition of painted *cassoni*, which by that time had largely gone out of fashion in Florence, where they were replaced by carved and partially gilt walnut chests that remained in vogue through the sixteenth century.

The panel illustrates the first half of the romance of Cupid and Psyche as told originally by Apuleius in *The Golden Ass* and later by Boccaccio in the *Genealogia deorum*. Beginning at the left, Psyche (who appears numerous times in the painting, always dressed in a flowing white gown) stands on the steps outside a palace with her two older sisters, while six suitors praise her beauty above that of Venus. In the sky above, the jealous Venus instructs Cupid to strike Psyche with love for a man of low estate, but Cupid instead falls in love with Psyche himself. In the distance at the left, Psyche is brought by her parents to consult an oracle concerning her marriage; she is instructed to be left alone at the summit of a mountain where she will encounter her future husband. In the center foreground, Psyche's weeping parents lead her up the path to the mountain, and at the top center she is shown alone and afraid at the summit. As she waits there, Zephyr, the west wind, blows her gently down into the valley, where she sleeps among the flowers and grasses. When she awakens she sees a marvellous palace but no servants. Entering, she dines and is wed to Cupid, whom she is not permitted to see. After some time has passed, she pleads with her husband to permit her to visit her sisters once again and, though he warns her against their jealousy, he has Zephyr bring them to the palace. Psyche's sisters, in the foreground at the far right, convince her that she is married not to a god but to a serpent. To the right of center in the foreground, the sisters are each given a small box of treasure from the palace and then returned to their own husbands. That night, defying his instructions not to try to learn his identity, Psyche holds an oil lamp above the sleeping Cupid and sees that he is indeed a god. A splash of hot oil from the lamp burns Cupid, who is shown fleeing in the top right corner; Psyche clings to his ankle and Cupid pushes her away in anger at her faithlessness. The concluding episodes from the story—in

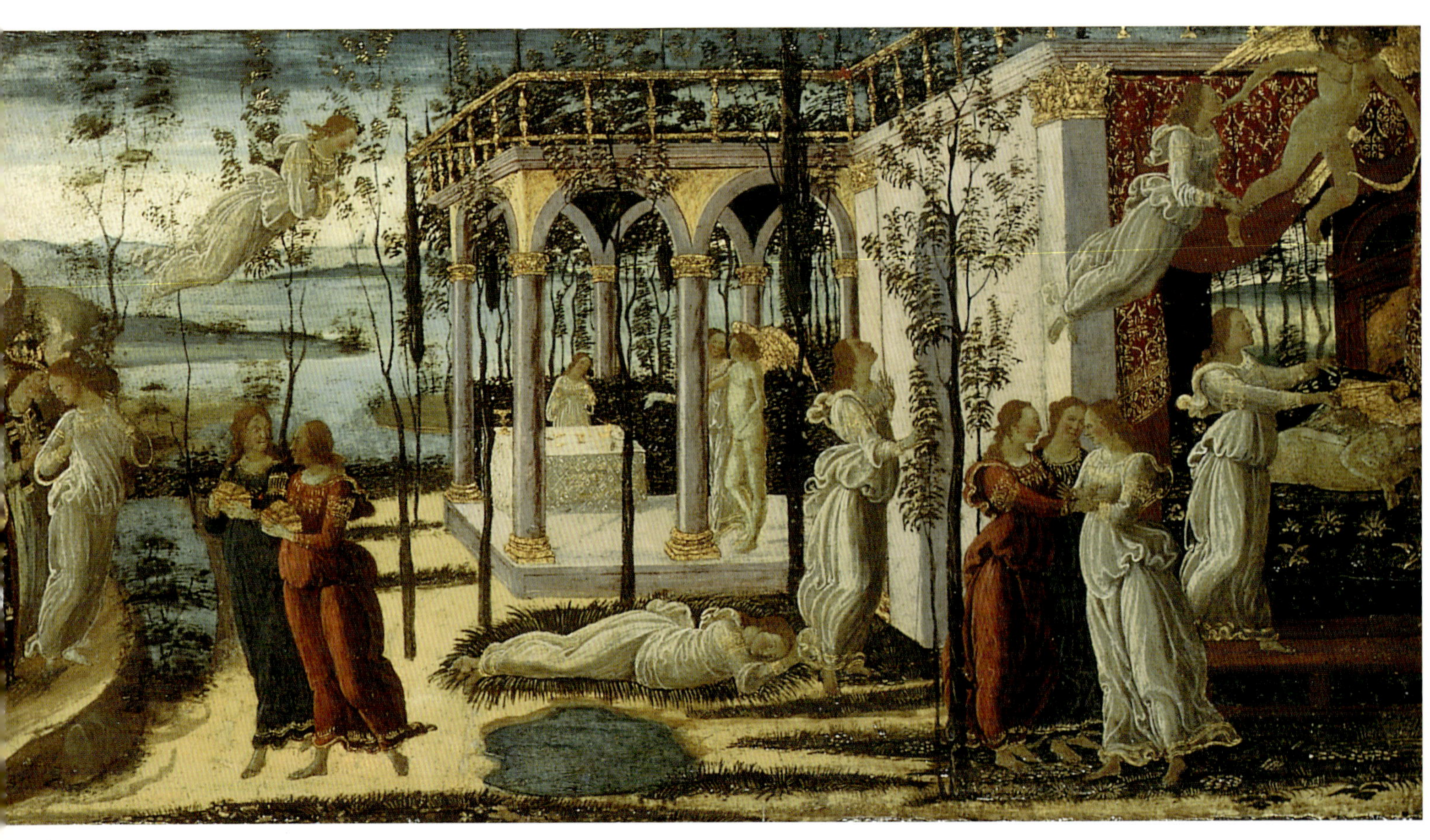

which Psyche endures numerous trials to demonstrate the worthiness of her love, appeases the anger of Venus, and is ultimately reunited with Cupid—are illustrated on another panel, undoubtedly cut from a companion chest, now in the Abegg collection in Riggisberg, Switzerland.

Though it could not have been painted by Botticelli himself, the Boston *Story of Psyche* does resemble his early narrative compositions, primarily in its figure and drapery style and in the mannerism of some of its poses. It was once attributed to Botticelli's pupil Filippino Lippi, the son of Fra Filippo Lippi, and dated around 1475, the moment at which Filippino is believed to have emerged from Botticelli's workshop as an independent craftsman. The grouping of figures in the left foreground of the Boston panel, however, appears to derive from Botticelli's fresco of *Moses and the Daughters of Jethro* painted in the Sistine Chapel in 1481–1482, while many of the costumes and poses throughout the panel relate to those in Botticelli's other two Sistine frescoes, the *Temptation of Christ* and the *Punishment of Korah, Dathan, and Abiram*. By this date, Filippino was painting in a fully mature style of his own, distinct from Botticelli's and not reconcilable with that of the Boston *Story of Psyche*. The latter has been attributed more convincingly to Jacopo del Sellaio, the head of an eclectic and heterogeneous workshop that specialized in the production of small devotional images and furniture panels such as this, frequently painted in imitation of better known and more fashionable painters, from Domenico Ghirlandaio to Botticelli and Filippino Lippi.

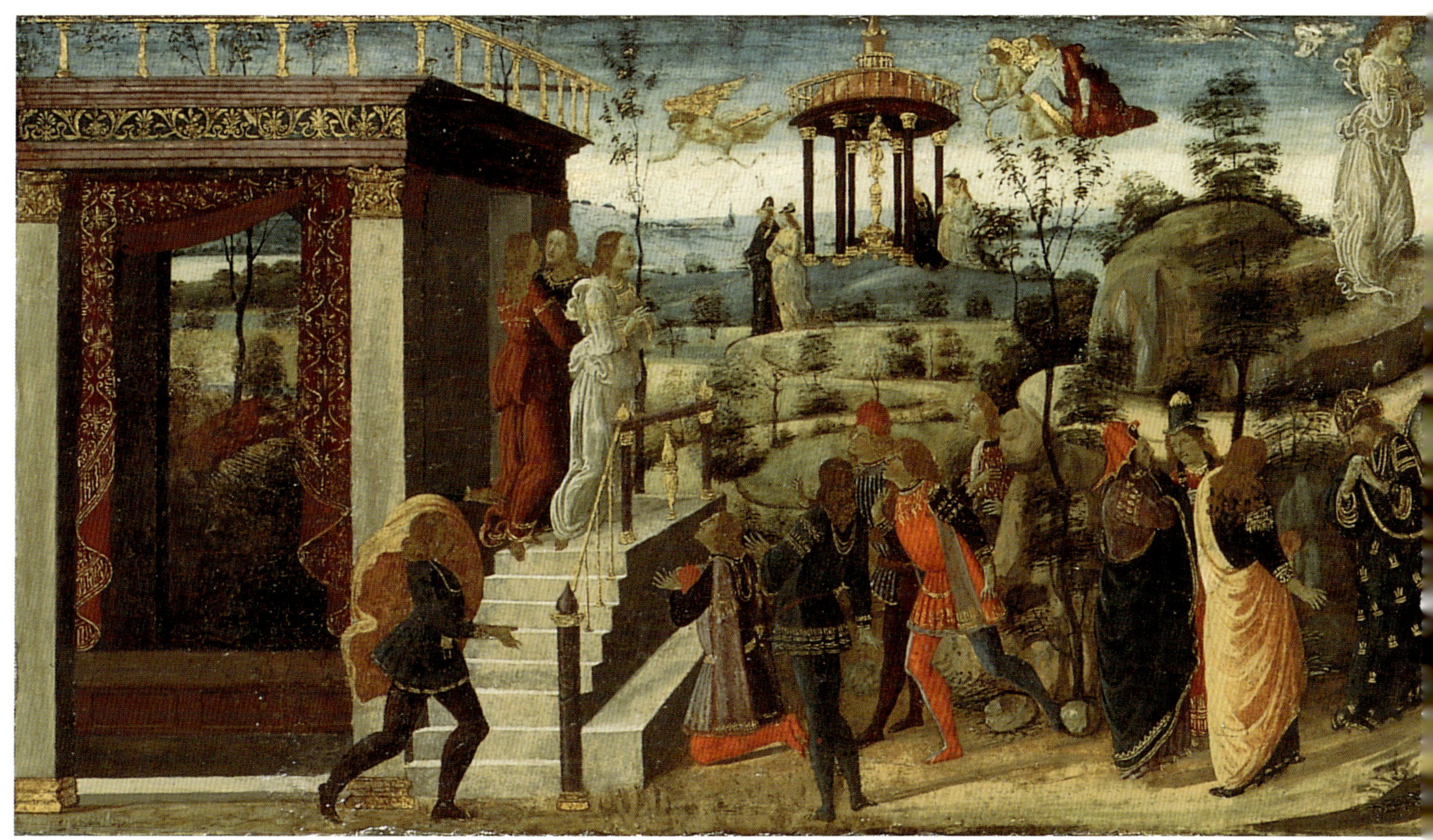

Catalogue 7

After a design by Sandro Botticelli (1445–1510)

The Assumption of the Virgin, ca. 1495–1500
Engraving
81.4 x 55.3 cm (32 x 21 3/4 in)
Museum of Fine Arts, Boston
James Fund, M26109

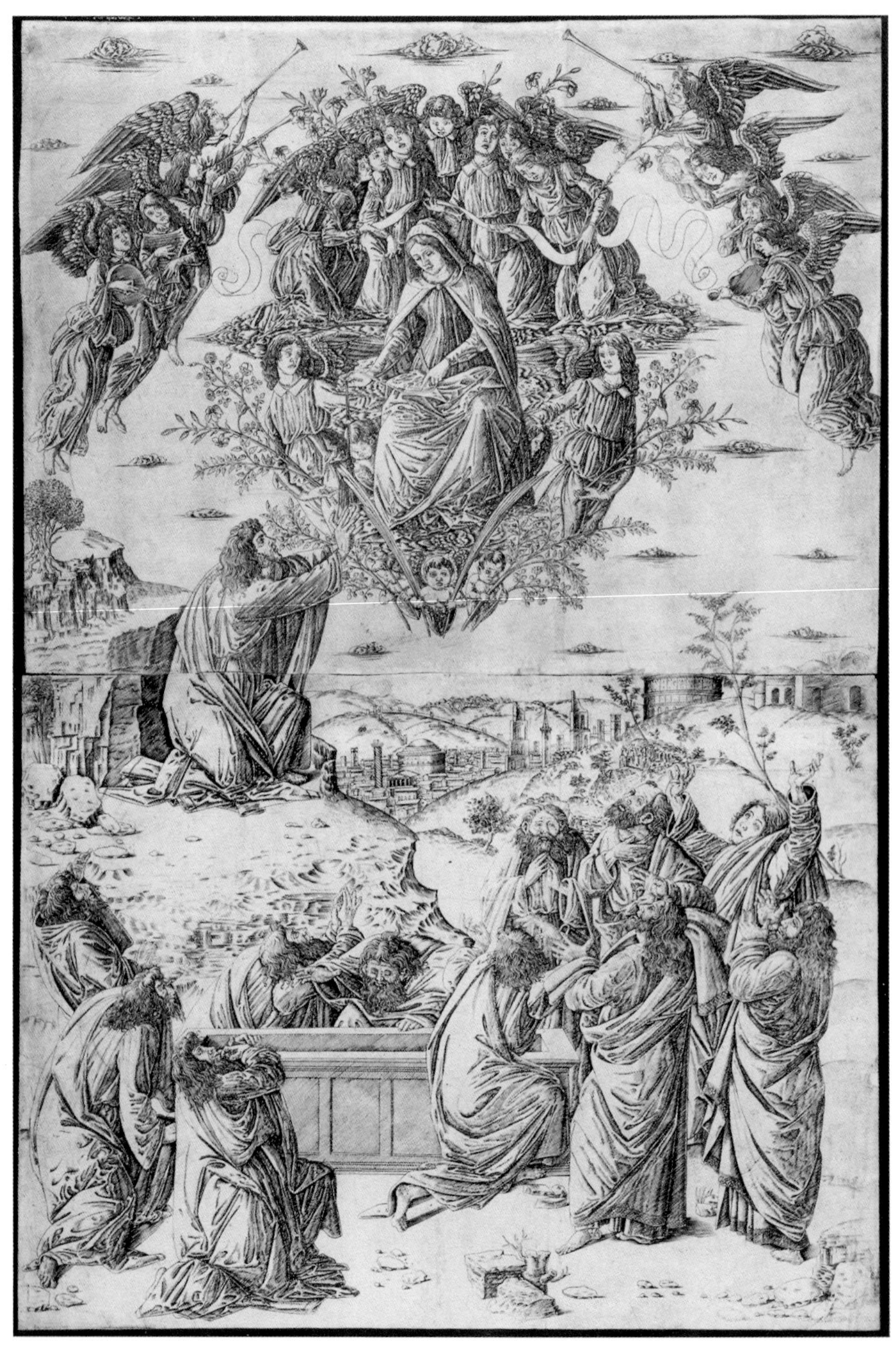

In Florence there seems to have been a well-respected tradition of one artist preparing drawings for another artist's work, especially of painters and sculptors working for artists in other media, such as intarsia, embroidery, engraving, and goldsmithing. Benvenuto Cellini, for example, in his *Treatise on Goldsmithing*, states that Antonio Pollaiuolo was a draughtsman "of such skill, that not only did all the goldsmiths make use of his excellent designs, but the sculptors and painters of the first rank also, and gained honor by them." According to Cellini, among those who profited most from this collaboration was Maso Finiguerra, master of the art of niello (small silver engravings popular in the mid-fifteenth century) "in which craft he had no rival, and he too always made use of the designs of the aforesaid Antonio." Vasari attributed to Maso Finiguerra the invention of the technique of copperplate engraving, a claim now known to be yet another of Vasari's chauvinistic exaggerations, but many of the designs for the earliest surviving Florentine engravings, if not their actual execution, are still associated with Maso's name.

According to Vasari, Maso was followed in the art of engraving by Baccio Baldini, a goldsmith, who is said to have relied on drawings by Botticelli for everything he made (see Cat. 2). In his biography of Botticelli, Vasari adds that "he [Botticelli] likewise engraved [*or had engraved*] many of the designs he had executed, but in a very inferior manner, the work being badly cut; the best attempt of this kind from his hand is the Triumph of the Faith by Fra Girolamo Savonarola." No impression of the *Triumph of the Faith* is known to exist (it must be assumed that only a relatively small percentage of early engraved images survive), nor is it possible to determine whether Botticelli might have engraved it himself or simply have supplied designs for it to a professional engraver, but numerous other prints, in addition to the illustrations to Landino's *Dante* of 1481 (Cat. 2), have been ascribed to Botticelli's invention. The difficulty with these attributions lies in seeing through the inevitable distortions of translation from one medium to another and determining the extent to which an engraver's personal style might mask that of his source. In the end, only two independent engravings are universally accepted as having been based on designs by Botticelli: a *Madonna and Child with Saints Helen and Michael* (impressions in the British Museum, London, and the Bibliothèque Nationale, Paris) and the large *Assumption of the Virgin* (examples in Berlin, Boston, Cleveland, Darmstadt, Florence, Hamburg, London, Paris, Rome, and Vienna).

Given Botticelli's prolific output and the success with which his designs were realized in intarsia (Urbino) and embroidery (Milan, Orvieto), it is likely that a number of other prints sometimes associated with his name were in fact worked up from his drawings. All of these attributions, however, relate to Botticelli's early style, which has much in common with that of other artists active in Florence in the 1460s and 1470s, and which was much imitated by minor painters and designers in the 1480s and 1490s. The attribution to Botticelli of the *Assumption of the Virgin* has never been contested primarily because it is clearly based on a late drawing by the artist, produced probably in the mid-1490s or possibly even around 1500, when his personal mannerisms had become so eccentric and exaggerated as to be unmistakable. The upper half of the composition, which is printed in two sheets, was developed from ideas first explored in the tondo of the *Virgin and Child with Angels and a Kneeling Saint John the Baptist* now in the Galleria Borghese, and in the altarpiece of the *Coronation of the Virgin* now in the Uffizi, both works generally dated around 1490. The lower half of the composition reflects the more tormented figure style typical of the artist's work at the end of that decade (see Cat. 10), and it may well have been designed at a significantly later date than the upper half. If so, the distant view of Rome in the center of the composition and the figure of Saint Thomas kneeling on the hilltop, which is rendered on a larger scale than any other figure in the print, may have been contrived at that time to elide the two halves more successfully. A drawing for this figure survives in the Biblioteca Ambrosiana, in Milan, but no drawings for any other parts of the print are known.

The Assumption of the Virgin, still one of the major feasts of the Church calendar (August 15), was a theme commonly represented in Florentine art in the Renaissance. Artists generally followed one of two standard compositions in treating the subject: the simpler version shows the Virgin floating in a glory of angels above her empty tomb, which is sometimes filled with roses; the more complex exposition, first developed in the fourteenth century, relates two separate events, the death or burial of the Virgin and her Assumption. In this latter version of the image, which was always divided into upper and lower halves, the Apostles appear below, clustered around the Virgin's tomb or bier, where her body generally lies prone; they are accompanied by a figure of Christ holding what appears to be a small child, a symbol of the Virgin's soul. In the sky above the Virgin ascends in glory, as in Fra Angelico's reliquary panel exhibited in the Early Italian Room at the Isabella Stewart Gardner Museum. Sometimes, as in Botticelli's print, the Virgin is shown lowering her sash to Saint Thomas, an important event for local devotions since the much-venerated relic of the Virgin's sash was preserved in the Cathedral of nearby Prato. Botticelli, however, has effectively created a new composition by redesigning the lower half not as a discrete event but as part of the larger scene of Assumption, depicting the bewildered Apostles staring in awe and wonder at the vision above them or in amazement at the empty tomb in their midst. It was in this more dramatic form that a majority of sixteenth-century artists would approach the subject, not impossibly in response to the example of Botticelli's invention.

The execution of Botticelli's *Assumption of the Virgin* is now recognized to be the work of the miniaturist and engraver Francesco Rosselli (1448–1508/13), brother of the painter Cosimo Rosselli, one of Botticelli's colleagues working on the Sistine Chapel frescoes in 1481–1482. Francesco Rosselli, who was also famous in his day as a mapmaker, is generally credited with having engraved most of the prints formerly classified as "Broad Manner" (in distinction to the "Fine Manner" prints associated with the name Baccio Baldini; see Cat. 2), referring to a distinctive technique of shading with strong, deeply cut diagonal lines that mimics the effects of pen and ink drawings. The *Assumption* is sometimes thought to be among Rosselli's last works, and some scholars believe it was engraved with the help of an assistant because the bite of the engraver's burin is even deeper and the lines shorter and stronger than is usual in his prints. Francesco's workshop was inherited by his son Alessandro and it was inventoried at Alessandro's death in 1525. A double-sided copper plate representing the Ascension (sic) listed in that inventory is thought to be the plate used to print the two sheets comprising the print on exhibition here. Whether it was executed by Francesco alone or with the assistance of Alessandro, the *Assumption* is frequently cited as Rosselli's masterpiece, the fruit of his collaboration with an exceptional designer working in what was then still an experimental medium.

Catalogue 8

Sandro Botticelli (1445–1510)

Saint Mary Magdalene at the Foot of the Cross, ca. 1500

(also known as the *Mystical Crucifixion*)
Tempera on canvas
72.3 x 51.3 cm (28 1/2 x 20 1/4 in)
Fogg Art Museum
Harvard University Art Museums
Gift of the Friends of the Fogg Museum of Art Fund, 1924.27

The *Mystical Crucifixion*, as this painting is commonly known, has long been a puzzle to scholars trying to explain the meaning behind its curious and unprecedented imagery. Its ostensible subject, Saint Mary Magdalene embracing the foot of the Cross, is not unusual in Italian painting of the fourteenth and fifteenth centuries; it is generally construed as an emblem of the efficacy of penance for salvation. Other details of the *Mystical Crucifixion* are probably also meant as penitential symbols, but reading the painting, which is self-evidently an illustration to a precise but as yet unidentified text, has been complicated by its severely deteriorated condition. Like the *Christ the Redeemer* also in the collection of the Fogg Art Museum (Cat. 4), it was painted on an unprimed cloth support and has suffered extensive losses from flaking and abrasion as well as from the natural decay of pigments. Details, therefore, that might originally have been difficult to interpret for anyone unfamiliar with the painting's text are now doubly difficult. What, for example, is the animal that the angel at the right holds by its hind leg? And what type of animal creeps out from under the Magdalene's cloak at the far left?

Most scholars agree that the *Mystical Crucifixion* is in some fashion linked to the ideas of Fra Girolamo Savonarola, the more so as it is clearly the city of Florence that fills the left background of the picture (the Cathedral and its bell tower, the Baptistry, and the Palazzo Vecchio are all recognizable). In the clear sky above the city is an apparition of God the Father in glory and two faintly rendered angels bearing white shields with red crosses. The right half of the painting is filled with what appears to be billowing smoke and a stormy sky. Diminutive figures of devils hurl flaming brands to the earth while an angel in the foreground menaces a wild animal with a sword. Several scholars have identified this animal as a lion, emblem of the city of Florence, and therefore see the painting as a metaphor for Florence threatened with Divine vengeance and saved through faith and repentance. One scholar understood the painting to be an allegory of the death of Pope Alexander VI Borgia in 1503; another interpreted it as a votive of thanksgiving for the delivery of Florence from the threats of the pope's nephew, Cesare Borgia, two years earlier. (It has long been fashionable to read complex allegories of topical political events into details of Italian Renaissance paintings, especially Botticelli's; see Cat. 10). If the flames and smoke at the right are understood to be a natural, not a political, scourge, the painting could also refer to one of the many outbreaks of plague that swept through Florence in this period, most virulently between 1499 and 1502.

The most widely accepted interpretation of the *Mystical Crucifixion*, however, associates it with the text of a sermon preached by Savonarola on January 13, 1495, describing a vision of the renewal of the Church. In his vision, Savonarola saw a black cross inscribed "The Anger of God" hanging over the city of Babylon/Rome, while the sky rained down swords, knives, and stones in stormy darkness. He then saw a gold cross over the city of

Jerusalem, reaching from the earth to the sky and inscribed "The Mercy of God." Around it the weather was calm, the air clear. Savonarola also saw a quaking sword poised above Italy and angels arriving bearing red crosses. According to this interpretation, Botticelli's Florence is the New Jerusalem, the Magdalene is the penitent Church which has chased out corruption (the animal fleeing from beneath the Magdalene's robes which, if it is a wolf, might also be a symbol of heresy), while the animal at the right represents Vice from which both the city and the Church are freed by the angel.

The merits of this interpretation lie in some vague correspondences between Savonarola's prophecy and some of the salient details of the painting (such as the stormy sky at the right and the shields with red crosses borne by angels at the left) and in the presumption, almost universally endorsed, that Botticelli was profoundly influenced by Savonarola's preaching. But in his other works illustrating specific texts—the Uffizi *Calumny of Apelles*; the stories of Nastagio degli Onesti (Prado), Virginia (Bergamo), and Lucretia (Isabella Stewart Gardner Museum, see Cat. 10); the engravings for Dante's *Inferno* (Cat. 2); or the drawings for the entire *Divine Comedy* (Berlin, Vatican)—Botticelli is careful to follow his source as exactly as possible, and that is clearly not the case here. Nor is it certain that Botticelli was as fervent a supporter of Savonarola as is commonly assumed. In all likelihood the *Mystical Crucifixion* was not painted as an illustration to any particular sermon or prophecy of Savonarola, though it may have been commissioned by one of his followers and it may illustrate a lost treatise inspired by Savonarola's constant predictions of doom and exhortations to repentance. Moreover, if it was painted after Savonarola's execution in 1498, as most scholars believe and as seems to be correct, it may even have been necessary to disguise overt references to his writings.

Whether the meaning of the allegory behind the *Mystical Crucifixion* is in fact Savonarolan or stems from some other source may never be known. The true fascination of the painting, however, lies not in its specific interpretation but in what it reveals about the depths and sophistication of Botticelli's literary culture. More than any artist other than Leonardo da Vinci among his contemporaries, and comparable only to Michelangelo in the next generation, Botticelli seems to have moved comfortably and as a peer among the highest intellectual circles of Florentine society. It was he who regularly received commissions to paint learned subjects like the Calumny, the Primavera, the Mystical Nativity, and the Mystical Crucifixion. Even subjects of apparently straightforward interpretation, such as the Birth of Venus, Pallas and the Centaur, and the Last Communion of Saint Jerome, assume an air of deeper significance in Botticelli's hands. In this respect Botticelli seems today to be the personification of all that is enigmatic in a period that prized the subtlety of hidden meanings and valued paintings, by such artists as Luca Signorelli and Piero di Cosimo, whose themes may never be satisfactorily unravelled.

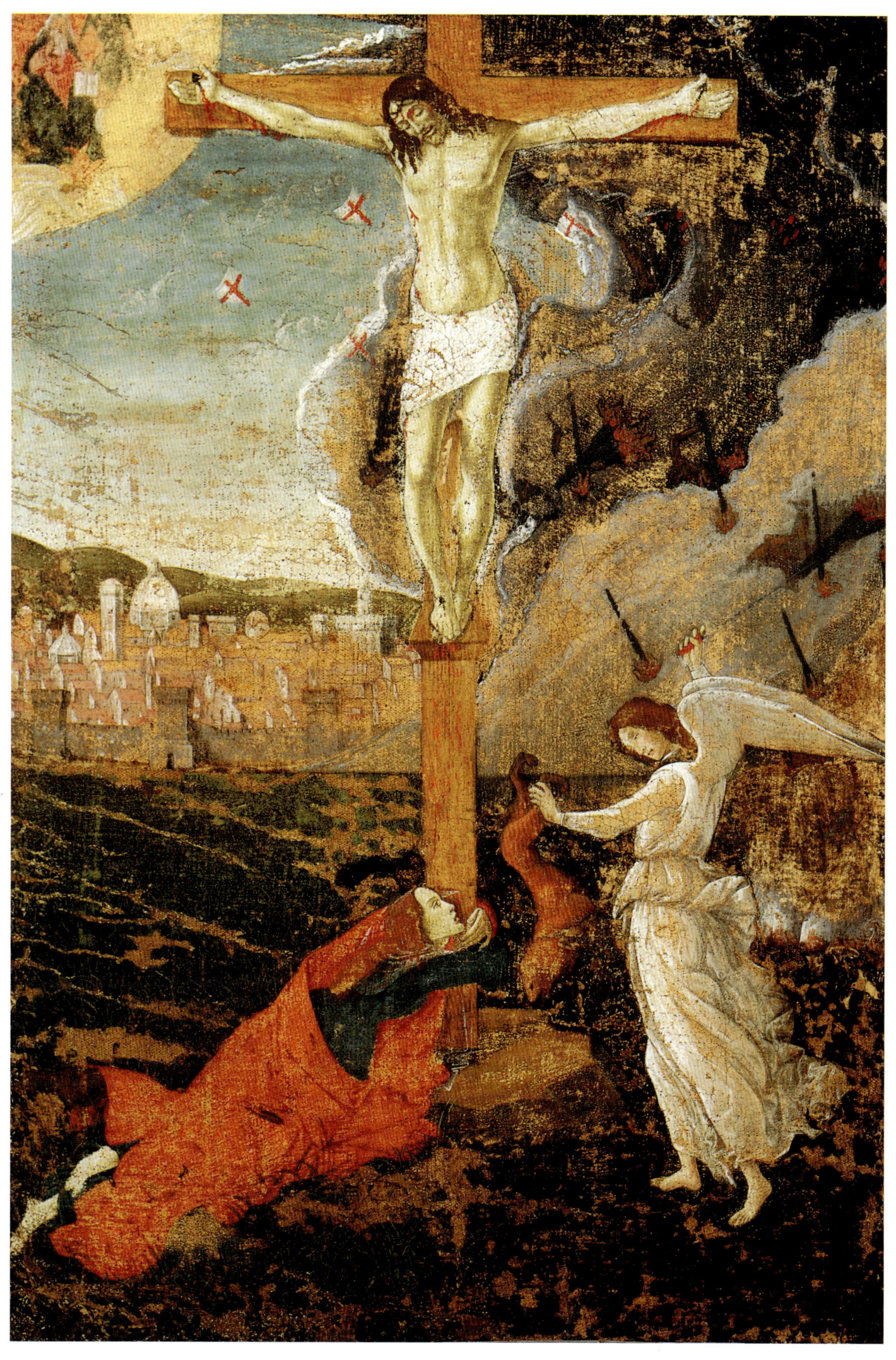

CATALOGUE 9

SANDRO BOTTICELLI (1445–1510)

Virgin and Child with the Young Saint John the Baptist, ca. 1500

Tempera on panel
123.8 x 84.4 cm (48 3/4 x 33 1/4 in)
Museum of Fine Arts, Boston
Sarah Greene Timmins Fund, 95.1372

This large and imposing panel was classed, through most of its known history, among the numerous Madonna and Child compositions believed to have been painted in Botticelli's studio by his assistants and followers, perhaps reproducing the design of a lost original by the master himself. Its large areas of flat, almost unmodulated color, its sharp outlines and inelegant proportions, and its stiff, almost brittle manner of rendering drapery folds were all considered typical of the efforts of Botticelli's imitators and copyists to translate into their own works the lyrical arabesques of Botticelli's draughtsmanship and the subtlety of his palette. Recently, however, it has been recognized that these same features are autograph characteristics of Botticelli's style in the last ten or fifteen years of his life, a period largely ignored in conventional studies of the artist's work. The Boston Madonna was certainly painted by Botticelli himself sometime around 1500, and it is instructive, aside from its inherent interest as a work of art, for what it reveals of Botticelli's working method at this late, understudied, and still underappreciated stage of his career.

The wood panel on which the Boston Madonna is painted is composed of four planks of wood glued and nailed together. Virtually the entire figural composition is contained on two vertical planks, with a third added across the bottom (rising to the level of the Virgin's knee and the cushion on which the Child sits) and a fourth extending the picture field at the right. Technical and visual evidence suggest that the last two planks were added to the main panel after work on a preliminary design had begun; indeed, seams marking their join to the main panel are plainly visible through the picture surface. Reduced to the area of its two original planks, the painting conforms in proportions and arrangement to a number of Madonna and Child compositions devised by Botticelli in the early 1490s. The drawing for it was probably invented at that time with a painting of this scale in mind; asked later to enlarge the composition, Botticelli evidently chose neither to order a fresh panel (simply tacking on additions to the existing one) nor to alter the cartoon (instead adding architectural details at the right-hand side and more of the Virgin's body at the bottom). The results, like much of Botticelli's late work, are unsettling: a highly eccentric spatial structure moving steeply backward towards the left; a sort of tabletop with a book mysteriously balanced against a large enamel vase; a cornice that serves no imaginable function wrapping around a partial wall; the Christ Child, the nominal subject of the painting, crowded inexplicably off-center to the left, on the lap of a disproportionately large and ungainly Virgin; and a beautifully rendered still life of roses that was first intended to be lilies (the freehand preparatory drawing for the lilies is now visible through thinning layers of paint above the vase at the upper right).

Two replicas of the Boston Madonna exist, both tondi. One, last recorded in the Lanckoroncki collection in Vienna (old photographs of this painting suggest that it is damaged and much restored, making it difficult to know whether it might be an original by Botticelli, a copy, or a workshop variant), follows the outlines of the composition as it must have looked before it was enlarged. The Virgin and Child are carefully centered, the Virgin's knees are not included so her proportions seem less exaggerated, spatial relationships are all clear and unambiguous, indications of architecture are minimal, and no still-life elements occupy the foreground. The other tondo, a much-damaged painting formerly in the Hay collection, is a free copy of the Boston panel, cropped at the corners to fill out a round shape but otherwise containing all the elements that contribute to the Boston Madonna's eccentricity. The sequence of permutations that this composition underwent, and the fact that as many as three versions of it survive, suggest that far from ceasing to paint altogether in his old age, as Vasari maintained, Botticelli perfected new ways to accommodate a continuing demand for his art. His studio may well have been smaller, but the vigor of his imagination and the power of his technique, as revealed in works like the Boston Madonna and the Gardner *Tragedy of Lucretia* (Cat. 10), were undiminished.

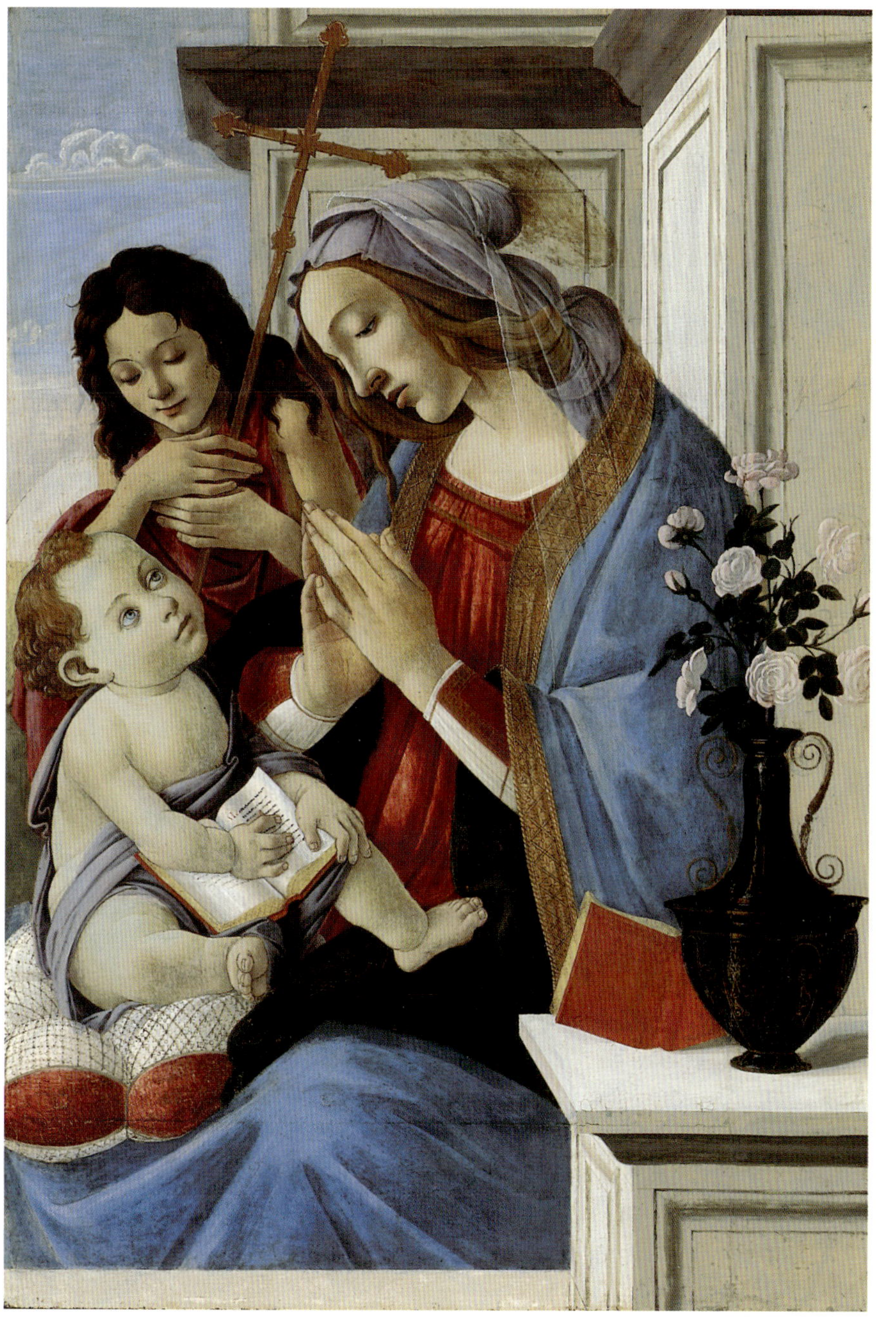

Catalogue 10

Sandro Botticelli (1445–1510)

The Tragedy of Lucretia, ca. 1500–1501
Oil on panel
83.8 x 176.8 cm (33 x 69 5/8 in)
Isabella Stewart Gardner Museum, Boston
P16e20

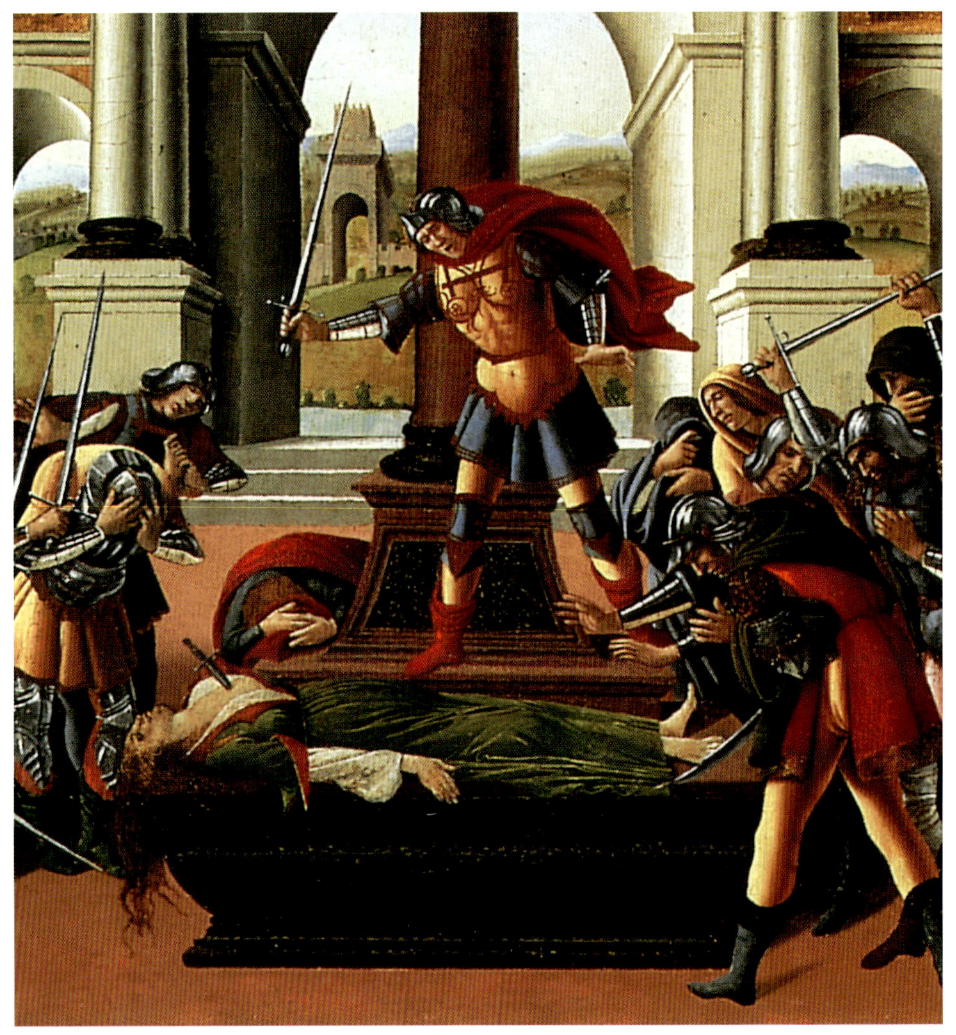

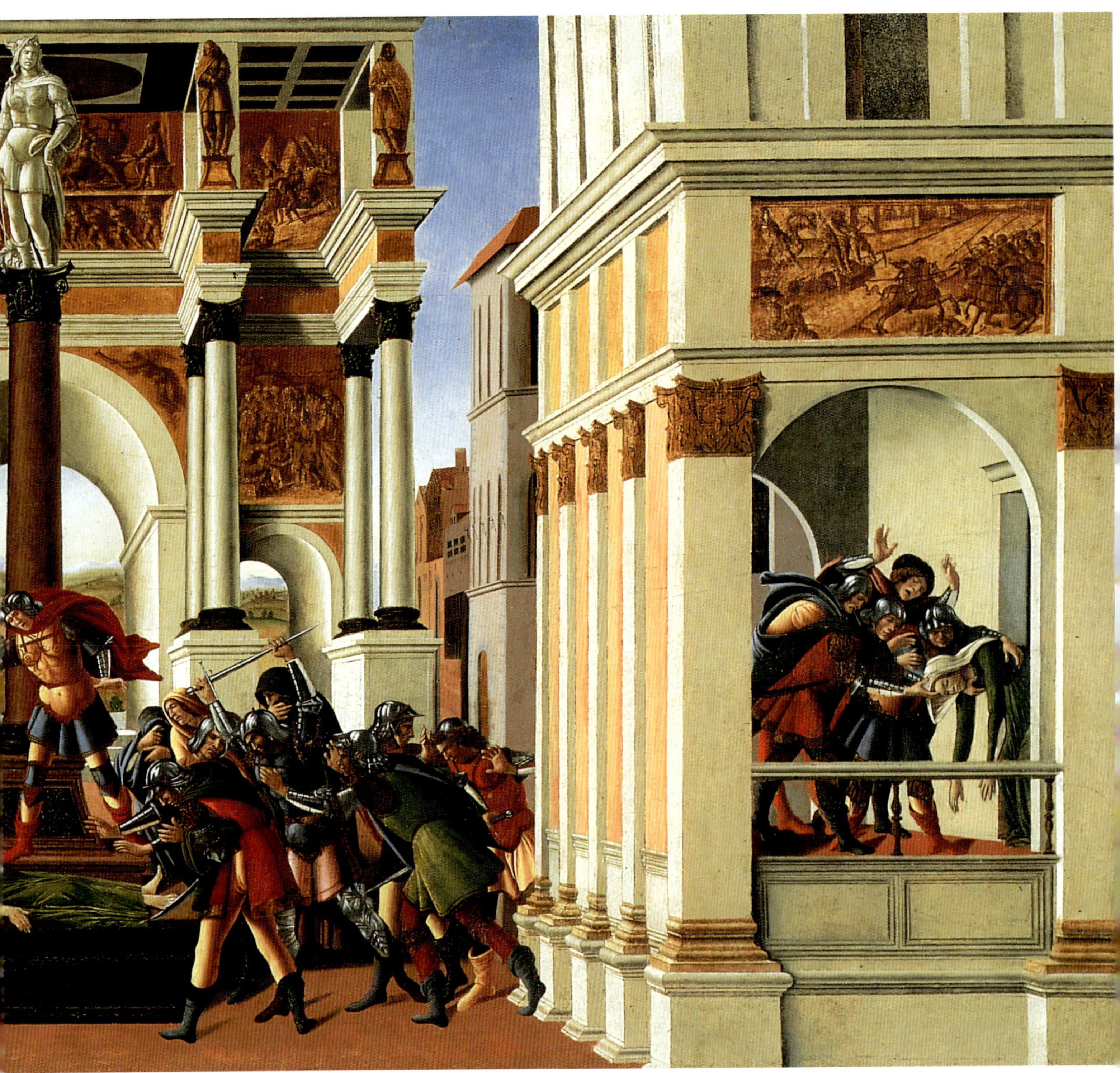

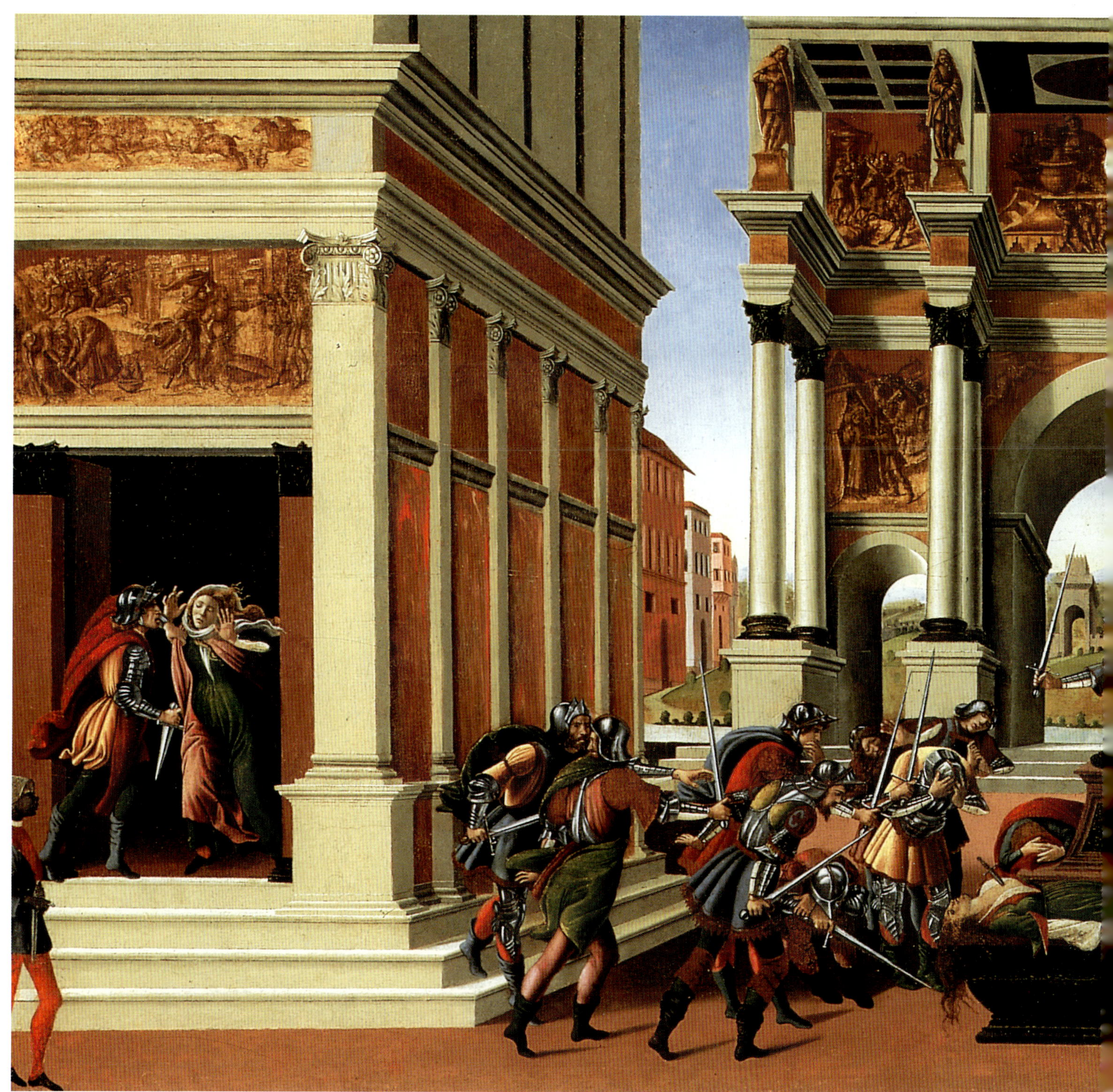

In the late fifteenth century it became fashionable among the highest circles of Florentine society to celebrate marriages by commissioning not only furniture (see Cat. 6) but also painted decorations filling the walls of an entire room. Rather than being executed directly on the walls in fresco, as had been the rule earlier, or woven into tapestries, as was the custom in the colder climates of Northern Europe, the biblical or classical stories chosen for these decorations were painted on wood panels which were then mounted as a frieze above the panelled wainscotting of the room, frequently surrounded by costly walnut moldings. Vasari describes two such commissions for which Botticelli was responsible. One comprised four panels recounting Boccaccio's story of Nastagio degli Onesti (three of these are now in the Museo del Prado, Madrid), painted to celebrate the marriage of Giannozzo di Antonio Pucci to Lucrezia Bini in 1482 or 1483. Another he described only generically: "In the Via de Servi and in the Palace of Giovanni Vespucci, which now belongs to Piero Salviati, this master painted numerous pictures around one of the chambers: they are enclosed within a richly decorated frame-work of walnut wood, and contain many beautiful and animated figures." The *Tragedy of Lucretia* in the Gardner Museum is often, and probably correctly, identified as one of the panels from the Palazzo Vespucci.

The Tragedy of Lucretia was a favorite subject of Renaissance painters and their patrons who admired it as a grand and tragic paradigm of the virtue of Chastity, a subject self-evidently appropriate for decorations commissioned in celebration of a wedding. The story, as told by Livy, Valerius Maximus, and Ovid, relates the consequences of the rape of Lucretia at knifepoint (shown in the scene at the left of the Gardner panel) by Sextus Tarquinius, son of King Tarquin of Rome. Lucretia, rather than live with the shame of her violation, stabbed herself to death (shown in the scene at the right of the panel) in the presence of her husband, Collatinus, her father, Spurius Lucretius, and two friends, Publius Valerius and Lucius Junius Brutus. Brutus vowed to avenge this deed, and in the scene at the center of the Gardner panel he is shown inciting a crowd of soldiers surrounding the bier of Lucretia to overthrow the corrupt Tarquin monarchy and restore the Republican Consuls of Rome.

Botticelli has disposed his scenes across an imaginary Roman forum that incorporates an improbable mixture of classical and Christian references. The building on the right, for example, is decorated with a frieze in its entablature showing the story of Horatius Cocles defending the bridge, and the Triumphal Arch closing off the foreground in the center is covered with reliefs illustrating stories of the heroism of Marcus Curtius and Mucius Scaevola. In front of the arch, however, stands a column surmounted by a statue of David with the head of Goliath, and the building at the left is decorated with the biblical story of Judith and Holofernes in its entablature frieze. The distant view of two streets and a landscape are also incongruous, for they introduce to a supposedly classical scene the architecture of fifteenth-century Florentine palaces and fortifications and, at the right, the Gothic facades of Netherlandish buildings. The latter are similar to those in the background of the *Madonna and Child* by Botticelli in the Fogg Art Museum.

A painting by Botticelli illustrating *The Story of Virginia* (Fig. 7), now in the Accademia Carrara at Bergamo, was undoubtedly painted as a pendant to the Gardner *Tragedy of Lucretia* and, like the Lucretia, it almost certainly came from the Palazzo Vespucci in Florence. Similar to the Gardner panel in size, shape, and style, it too portrays the rape of a virtuous woman, her death (this time at the hand of her father, who vowed to kill her rather than permit her to be further dishonored), and a subsequent call to revolt against the abuses of tyranny. Both these stories are encountered, sometimes as a pair, in earlier examples of painted *cassoni* and *spalliera* (as these wainscotting panels are known), where they were invariably intended as allegories of marital virtue. Early in the sixteenth century, however, Lucius Junius Brutus came to personify the struggles of republican government against tyranny, and the story of Lucretia became emblematic not of the virtue of Chastity but of a heroic self-sacrifice that led to the overthrow of the Tarquin regime, a theme that could be successfully adapted to the story of Virginia as well. As the stories of the two biblical tyrannicides David and Judith, which are incorporated into the background of the Gardner *Lucretia* also bear republican overtones, scholars have come to believe that the Vespucci panels were

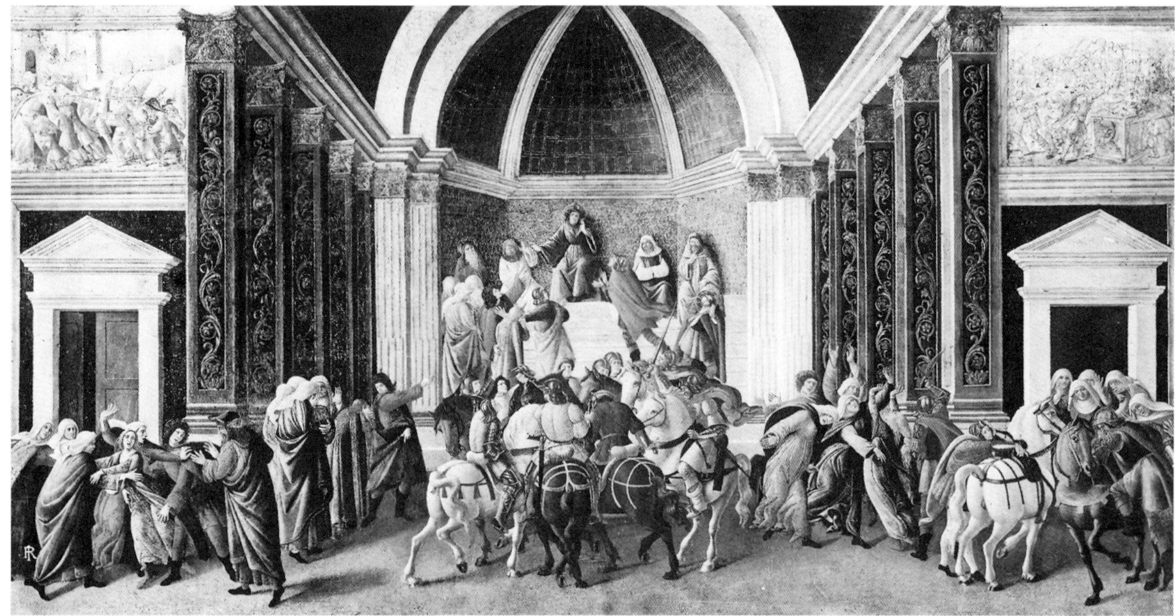

Figure 7. *The Story of Virginia.* Bergamo, Accademia Carrara.

painted as political allegories. This understanding has engendered a bewildering variety of explanations and interpretations of Botticelli's work, generally either anti-Medicean or anti-Savonarolan in nature. One scholar has even suggested that the Gardner *Lucretia* could not have been painted until after 1504, when the Florentine government removed Donatello's statue of Judith from its dominant position alongside the door of the Palazzo Vecchio, where it was originally placed to commemorate the expulsion of the Medici in 1492, replacing it with Michelangelo's colossal statue of David, for only this vicissitude of Florentine politics could account for the relative prominence of Judith and David in the background of Botticelli's painting.

Elaborate interpretive theories such as these shed more light on the enthusiasms of modern scholarship than on the intentions of painters or their clients in Botticelli's day. No detail of either the *Tragedy of Lucretia* or the *Story of Virginia* suggests that they were painted as anything but decorations in honor of a wedding. It is even possible to cite a precedent for the stories of Horatius Cocles and Mucius Scaevola that are painted on the Triumphal Arch behind Lucretia's bier; these two stories decorate the backs of a pair of *cassoni* ordered on the occasion of the marriage of Lorenzo Morelli and Vagia de' Nerli in 1472. If the Gardner and Bergamo panels were indeed those seen by Vasari in the palace of Giovanni Vespucci, which was purchased only in 1499 by Giovanni's father, Guidantonio, they would in all likelihood have been commissioned in celebration the following year of Giovanni Vespucci's marriage to Namicina di Benedetto Nerli, a kinswoman of Vagia de' Nerli, for whom the 1472 chests had been painted.

The elaborate architectural setting of the Gardner *Lucretia* has been explained as an imitation of theatrical backdrops that were designed according to Vitruvius' instructions for the proper staging of Tragedy. It is possible that Botticelli intended a conscious reference to Vitruvius, a reference that would have been understood by the better-educated among his contemporaries, but it is equally possible that he was simply following a formula devised earlier in the fifteenth century by his fellow Florentine Leon Battista Alberti. The specific source is less important than the fact that throughout his career Botticelli employed detailed backgrounds of classical and contemporary architecture, carefully rendered in convincing linear perspective, in paintings of every scale and subject from the Sistine Chapel frescoes to his humblest and most repetitive Madonna and Child compositions. The care with which these backgrounds are invariably defined contrasts with Botticelli's cavalier attitude towards landscape, as reported by no less an authority than Leonardo da Vinci. Leonardo wrote, in his *Treatise on Painting* of about 1492, that some painters very little esteemed landscape, " . . . as our Botticello, who said that such a study was vain, since by merely throwing a sponge full of divers colors against a wall, it left on the wall a stain wherein was seen a fine landscape." Such a remark sounds more like an example of Botticelli's famously caustic sense of humor than of his actual painting practice, though it is suggestive of the relative value he assigned to the many tasks a successful artist needed to master. Clearly he valued the study of architecture very highly, yet he was not so scrupulous in his studies that he felt it necessary to rationalize the alternating stripes of light and shadow on the upper stories of the buildings in the left and right foreground of the *Tragedy of Lucretia*, or to provide either of those buildings with windows on the ground floor.

The style of Botticelli's paintings from the last decade of his life, beginning with such works as the Gardner *Tragedy of Lucretia* and the *Mystical Nativity* in the National Gallery, London, is dramatically different from that of his earliest career. The gentle calligraphy of his earlier drawing and the balletic grace of his figure types, derived from Filippo Lippi but perfected in his own unmistakable idiom, have given way to hard, almost engraved lines and crabbed, intensely over-wrought figures. The delicate veils of color that warmed the atmosphere and created a sense of open space as well as of surfaces and textures in paintings like the *Chigi Madonna* (Cat. 1) have become adamantine blocks of bright, unmodulated tone, lending a cold clarity to a light that defines figures and architecture with somewhat inconsistent results (note, for instance, that the soldiers in the center of the *Tragedy of Lucretia* cast shadows along the ground at differing angles of illumination and not at all against the base of the building at the right). In part this change may be attributable to Botticelli's shift to the fashionable medium of oil paints, a shift he was apparently never comfortable making, having been one of the century's greatest technicians in the use of tempera paints. Scholars have also seen in the stiffening of Botticelli's late style proof of Vasari's claim that the artist was physically debilitated at the end of his life: "Finally, having become old, unfit for work, and helpless, he was obliged to go on crutches, being unable to stand upright, and so died, after long illness and decrepitude." Whether this story be fact or fiction, Botticelli's late works betray no perceptible diminution in his power of expression or in his compositional genius. The Gardner *Tragedy of Lucretia* is certainly one of the great masterpieces of Florentine painting from the last years of probably its greatest period, the golden age of the fifteenth century.

Appendix to Catalogue 2

Nineteen engraved illustrations to the *Inferno* of Dante Alighieri,
appearing in *La Commedia di Dante* with a commentary by Cristoforo Landino,
published in Florence, 1481, by Niccolo di Lorenzo della Magna
41.1 x 26.6 cm (16 1/4 x 10 1/2 in)
Bound book
Isabella Stewart Gardner Museum, Boston
2.c.1/8

Canto Illustrations

Titles are given as they appear in *Early Italian Engraving*,
by Arthur M. Hind, Vol. I, London, 1938

I. Dante Lost in the Wood, Escaping, and Meeting Virgil

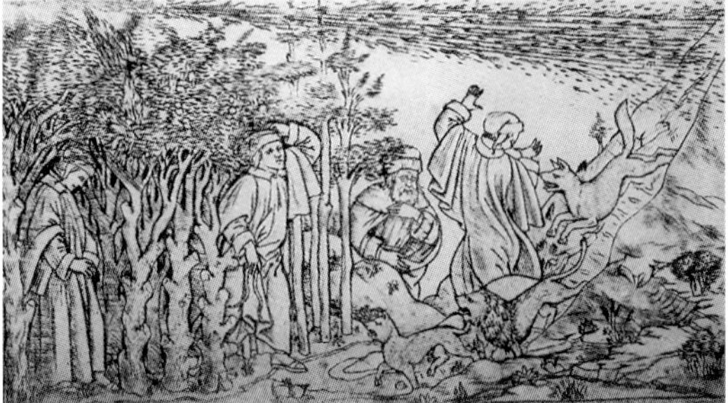

II. Dante and Virgil, with the Vision of Beatrice

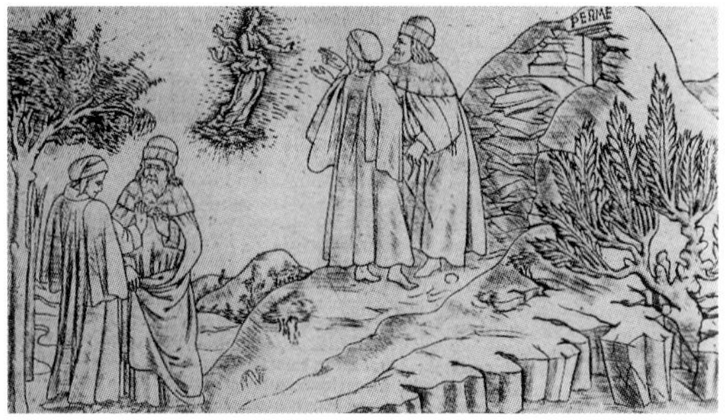

III. Dante and Virgil at the Entrance to Hell: Acheron and Charon's Boat

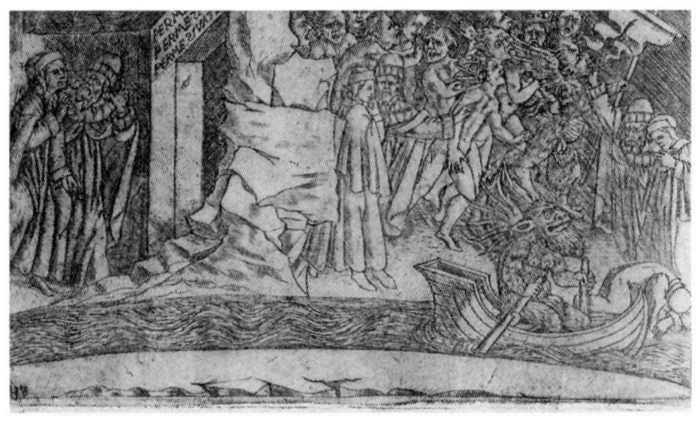

IV. Dante Awakening and Discoursing with Ancient Sages and Warriors in Limbo

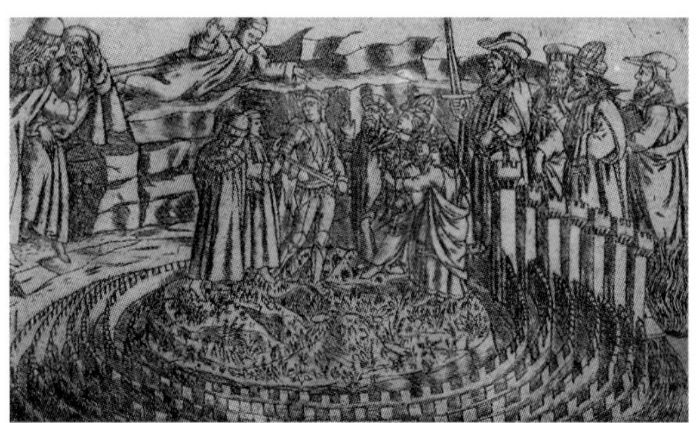

V. The Judgment Seat of Minos: The Punishment of Lust

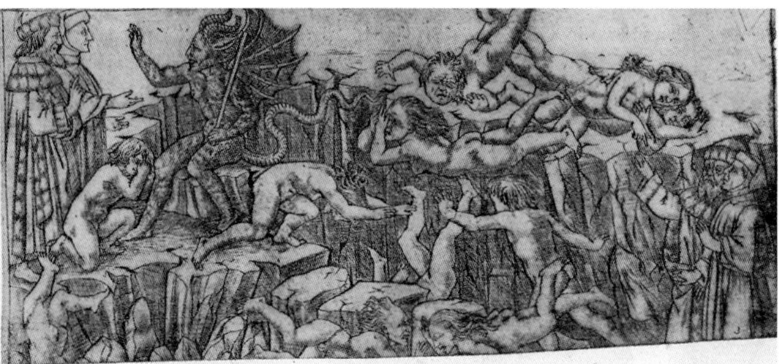

VI. Cerberus: The Punishments of Gluttony

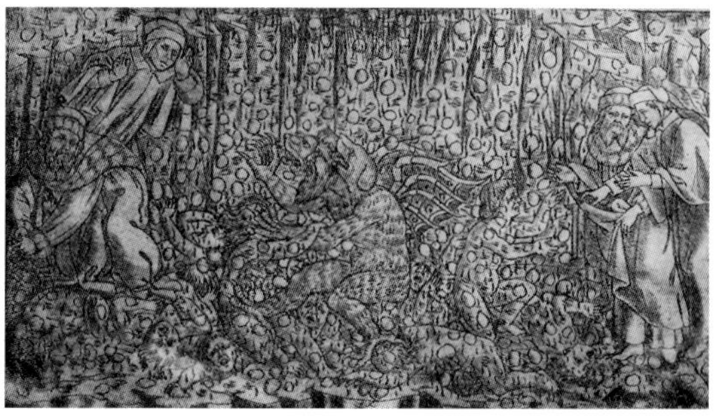

VII. Plutus: The Punishment of Avarice and Waste

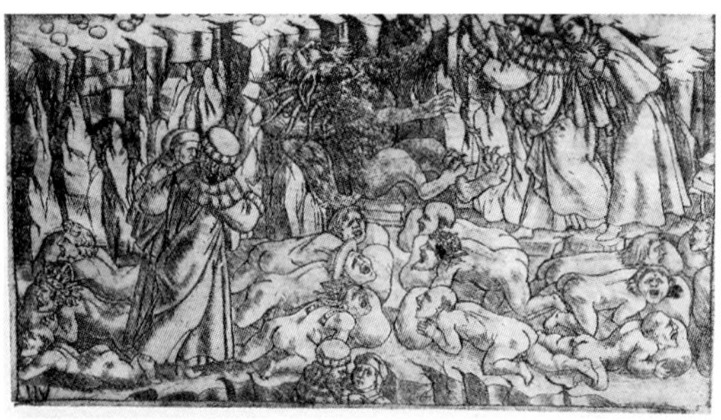

VIII. The Styx, with the Punishments of Wrath; The Boat of Phlegyas and House of Dys

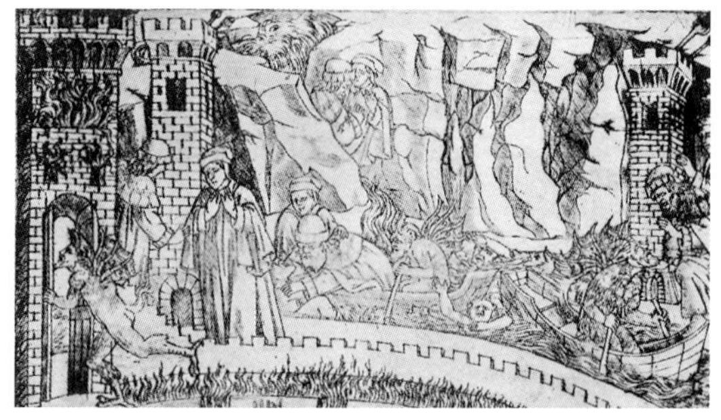

IX. The Styx and the City of Dys: The Furies and Medusa: The Protecting Angels

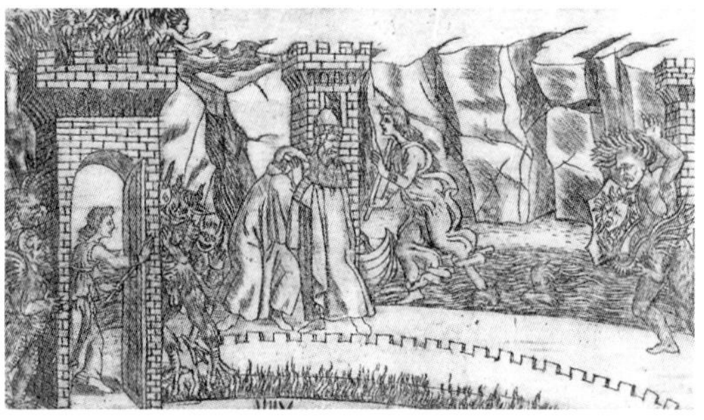

X. The City of Dys, and the Punishments of Heresy

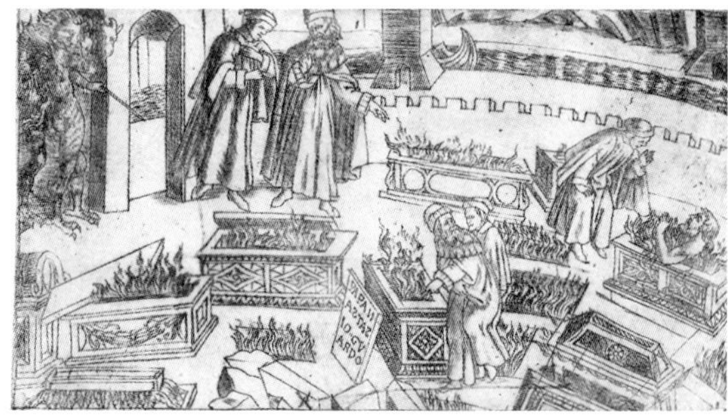

XI. Refuge Beside the Tomb of Pope Anastasius; Descent Towards the Seventh Circle

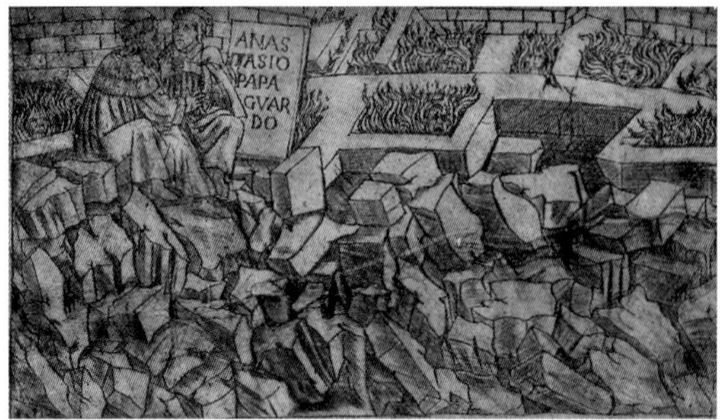

XII. The Minotaur: The Centaurs and the Punishment of Murder

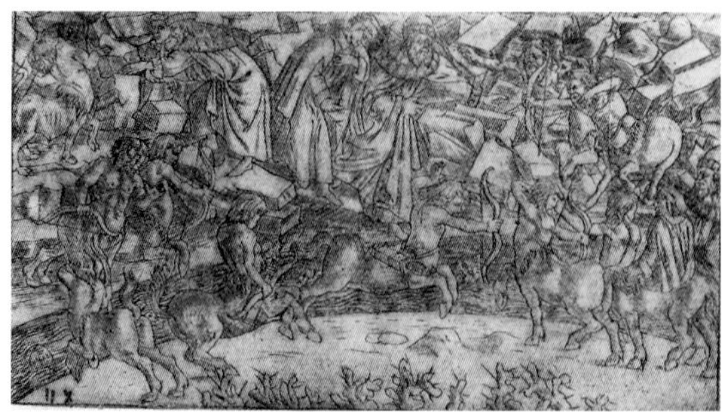

XIII. The Thorny Wood: The Harpies: The Punishments of Suicide

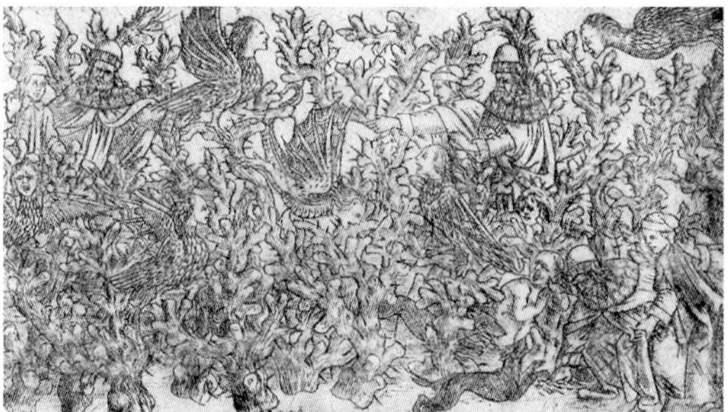

XIV. The Rain of Fire: The Punishments of Outrage and Blasphemy: Capaneus: The Banks of the Phlegethon

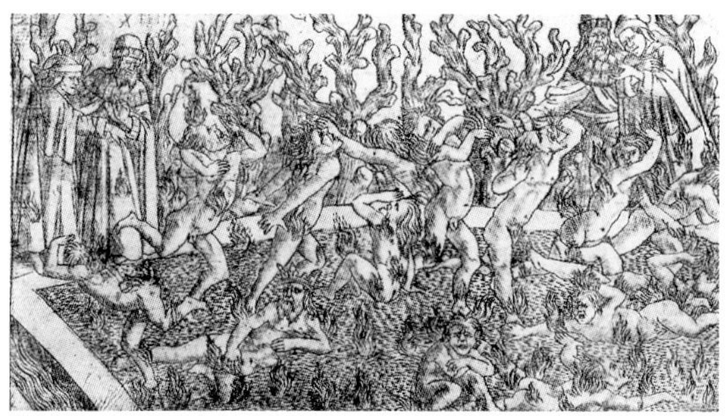

XV. The Rain of Fire and the Banks of the Phlegethon: The Punishment of Sodomy: Brunetto Latini

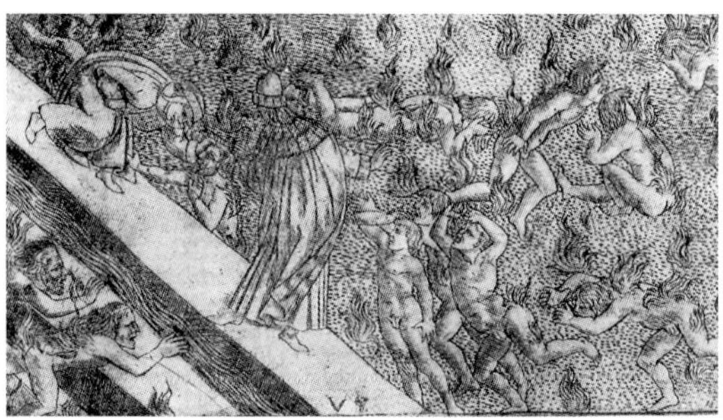

XVI. The Banks of Phlegethon: The Punishments of Sodomy: The Cord Dropped into the Pit: Geryon

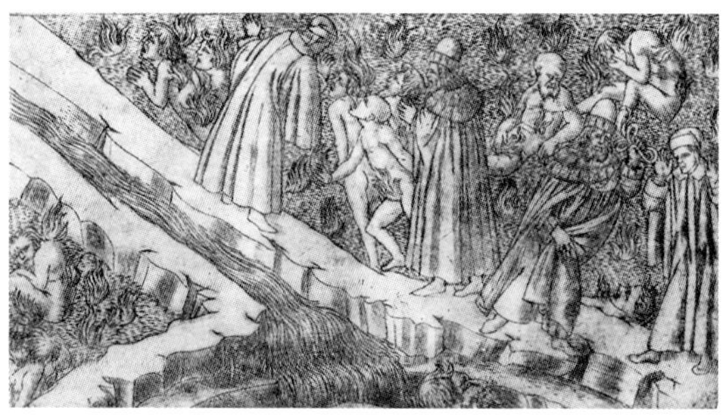

XVII. The Punishments of Usury: Geryon and the Descent into the Eighth Circle

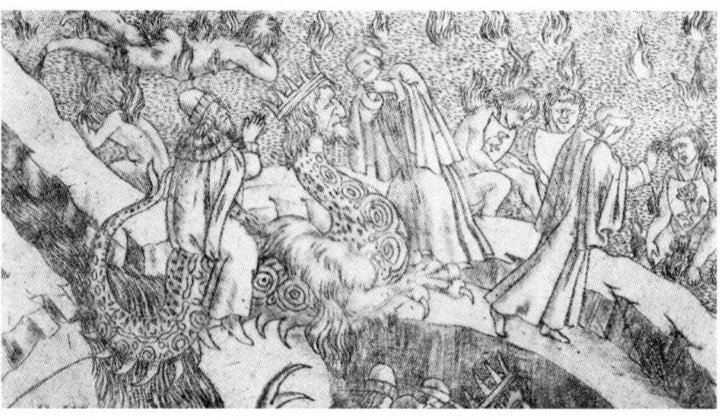

XVIII. The Departure of Geryon: The Malebolge: The Punishments of Pandering and Flattery

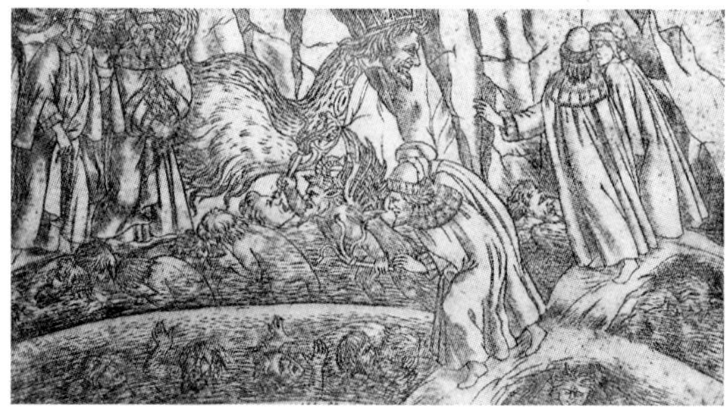

XIX. The Malebolge Continued: The Punishments of Simony

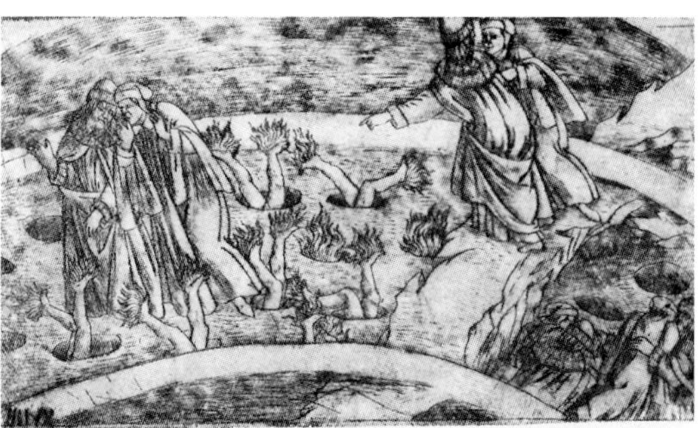

Checklist of the Exhibition

Please note that for all dimensions, height precedes width and that when an area is irregular, the maximum height or width is given.

1
Sandro Botticelli (1445–1510)
Madonna and Child with an Angel, ca. 1472–1475
(also known as the *Chigi Madonna*
or the *Madonna of the Eucharist*)
Tempera on panel
85.2 x 65 cm (33 1/2 x 25 5/8 in)
Isabella Stewart Gardner Museum, Boston
P27w73

2a
La Commedia di Dante with a commentary by Cristoforo Landino, published in Florence, 1481, by Niccolo di Lorenzo della Magna
Bound book with engraved illustrations
41.1 x 26.6 cm (16 1/4 x 10 1/2 in)
Isabella Stewart Gardner Museum, Boston
2.c.1/8

2b
After a design by Sandro Botticelli (1445–1510)
Dante Lost in the Wood, Escaping, and Meeting Virgil
(illustration to the *Inferno*, Canto I)
Engraving
9.5 x 17.4 cm (3 3/4 x 6 5/8 in)
Harvard University Art Museums
Gray Collection of Engravings Fund
G7835

2c
After a design by Sandro Botticelli (1445–1510)
Dante and Virgil, with the Vision of Beatrice
(illustration to the *Inferno*, Canto II)
Engraving
9.6 x 17.4 cm (3 3/4 x 6 5/8), includes text of entire page
Fogg Art Museum
Harvard University Art Museums
Gift of Paul J. Sachs
M667

3
Sandro Botticelli (1445–1510)
The Nativity, ca. 1482–1485
Tempera and oil on panel
79.6 cm (31 5/8 in) diameter
Isabella Stewart Gardner Museum, Boston
P27e1

4
Sandro Botticelli (1445–1510) and Studio
Christ the Redeemer (Salvator Mundi), ca. 1490
Tempera on linen
57.1 x 34.9 cm (22 1/2 x 13 3/4 in)
Fogg Art Museum
Harvard University Art Museums
Gift of the Friends of the Fogg Museum of Art Fund
1930.2

5
Francesco Botticini (1446–1497)
Virgin and Child with the Young Saint John the Baptist, ca. 1470–1480
Tempera on panel
67 x 47.3 cm (26 1/4 x 18 1/2 in)
Isabella Stewart Gardner Museum, Boston
P16w21

6
Jacopo del Sellaio (1441/2–1493)
The Story of Psyche, ca. 1490
Tempera and oil on panel
42 x 151.8 cm (16 9/16 x 59 3/4 in)
Museum of Fine Arts, Boston
Picture Fund
12.1049

7
After a design by Sandro Botticelli (1445–1510)
The Assumption of the Virgin, ca. 1495–1500
Engraving
81.4 x 55.3 cm (32 x 21 3/4 in)
Museum of Fine Arts, Boston
James Fund
M26109

8
Sandro Botticelli (1445–1510)
Saint Mary Magdalene at the Foot of the Cross,
ca. 1500
(also known as the *Mystical Crucifixion*)
Tempera on canvas
72.3 x 51.3 cm (28 1/2 x 20 1/4 in)
Fogg Art Museum
Harvard University Art Museums
Gift of the Friends of the Fogg Museum
of Art Fund
1924.27

9
Sandro Botticelli (1445–1510)
Virgin and Child with the Young Saint John the Baptist,
ca. 1500
Tempera on panel
123.8 x 84.4 cm (48 3/4 x 33 1/4 in)
Museum of Fine Arts, Boston
Sarah Greene Timmins Fund
95.1372

10
Sandro Botticelli (1445–1510)
The Tragedy of Lucretia, ca. 1500–1501
Oil on panel
83.8 x 176.8 cm (33 x 69 5/8 in)
Isabella Stewart Gardner Museum, Boston
P16e20